READY 2 GO

To order additional copies of
Ready 2 Go
by Randy Fishell, call **1-800-765-6955**.

Visit us at
www.AutumnHousePublishing.com
for information on other Autumn House® products.

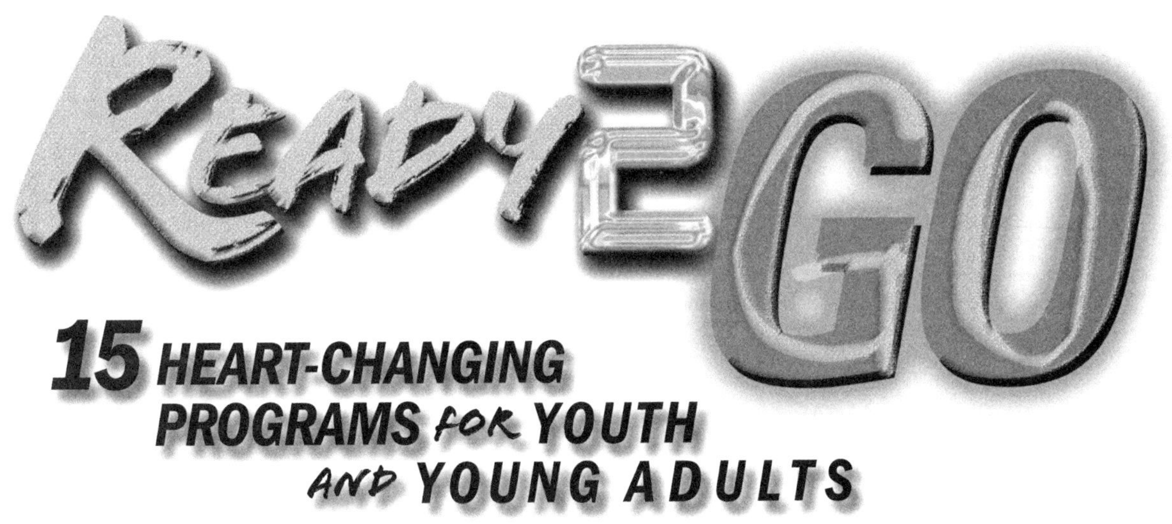

RANDY FISHELL

Published by Autumn House® Publishing, a division of Review and Herald® Publishing, Hagerstown, MD 21741-1119

Autumn House® titles may be purchased in bulk for educational, business, fund-raising, or sales promotional use. For information, please e-mail SpecialMarkets@reviewandherald.com.

Autumn House® Publishing publishes biblically based materials for spiritual, physical, and mental growth and Christian discipleship.

The author assumes full responsibility for the accuracy of all facts and quotations as cited in this book.

This book was
Edited by Penny Estes Wheeler
Designed by Ron J. Pride
Cover photos © PhotoDisc
Interior designed by Heather Rogers
Typeset: Bembo 12/17

PRINTED IN U.S.A.

12 11 10 09 08 5 4 3 2 1

Library of Congress Cataloging-in-Publication Data
Fishell, Randy.
Ready to go!: 15 heart-changing programs for youth and young adults/Randy Fishell.
p. cm.
Includes bibliographical references.
1. Church work with youth. 2. Church work with young adults. I. Title.
BV4447.F585 2008
268'.433—dc22
2008005142

ISBN 978-0-8127-0459-4

Contents

Preface

One of my hobbies is Civil War relic hunting. One of my buddies told me recently, "Relic hunting must be kinda like fishing on land."

I love finding buried treasure with my metal detector. Similarly, my hope is that the programs in this book will lead you and your group's participants to discover buried *spiritual* treasure.

These programs are crafted to take participants deeper into God's Word and each other's lives. The programs may be tailored to your allotted time frame. If it appears that a program may run overtime, either eliminate one of the activities (usually the last one) or continue the program at the next gathering. If, on the other hand, you need more material to fill some time, just turn to the Discussion Questions or Suggested Scripture section for each program. Both provide further insight on that program's topic.

Programs 11 through 15 are especially suitable for college-age young adults, but also contain appropriate ideas for mature high school groups.

Best of success as you strive to bring a clear, creative picture of the Christian way of life to youth and young adults.

RANDY FISHELL

FEAR

1

Fear Today, Gone Tomorrow

PURPOSE

To show that God stands ready to assist us in dealing positively with fear.

MATERIALS NEEDED

3" x 5" index cards, pencils
whiteboard or newsprint
cement block and rope (for optional activity *Near Miss*)
motorcycle helmet with face shield or chin guard

PREPARATION

Give a pencil and index card to several group members as they enter. Ask them to write down a time in their past that they feared something that turned out to be harmless. This information will be shared in the activity *Hindfright*.

For the optional activity, *Near Miss*, loop a rope through one end of a cement block and securely suspend the assembly from a ceiling beam so that the block hangs at chest level. *Note: the block must be totally unobstructed, as it will swing in pendulum fashion.*

On the whiteboard or newsprint, write down the phobias found in the Interaction section. *(Cover them, or turn the board around until needed.)*

Introduction

SAY: Someone has suggested that the two unavoidable things in life are death and taxes. There is something else though that seems inevitable: fear. From the womb to the tomb, this unwelcome emotion pays an occasional visit to every person.

Not all fear is bad. In fact, some situations call for extra adrenaline. These are rational fears. But at other times feeling afraid is merely a by-product of a skewed perception of reality. When this happens, a person's discomfort is the result of an irrational fear. Most of us can probably recall a time we exhibited irrational fear.

Activity: *Hindfright*

Ask the previously selected group members to tell about their situations of unwarranted fear. (Allow for others to tell about their fears as time permits.) The experience will help to create an atmosphere of openness. It also points out that our irrational fears come in many forms.

Optional Activity: *Near Miss* *(See above for activity preparation.)*

This experience demonstrates the reality of irrational fear.

Ask for a volunteer who is willing to face some potential discomfort. However, assure them that they will not be injured. Have the volunteer put on the motorcycle helmet and leather jacket, then stand with heels against a wall. Draw the cement block up to the participant's chest, and inform them that the cement block will be released from that point and allowed to swing back completely. Explain that as long as they stand perfectly still, it is impossible to be hurt by the return swing of the block.

The law of physics prevents the block from returning beyond the original point of release. But usually, even when this is fully explained, most participants will experience a last-second twinge of discomfort. This is irrational fear.

Interaction

SAY: For some of us irrational fears can spawn an avoidance pattern. We'll avoid any situation that might allow us to encounter the noxious stimulus. When this happens, we're said to have a phobia.

The term *phobia* may sound threatening. However, it's a common condition. Here are some phobias found in American society. (Reveal the technical names written on the whiteboard, and ask the group members to identify the fear it describes. Then go through the list, asking for responses and supplying definitions as necessary.)

1. Acrophobia—fear of heights
2. Claustrophobia—fear of confining spaces
3. Xenophobia—fear of strangers
4. Agoraphobia—fear of open spaces, or fear of a reaction to fear itself (such as a panic attack)
5. Zoophobia—fear of animals
6. Musophobia—fear of mice
7. Nyctophobia—fear of night or darkness
8. Androphobia—fear of men
9. Gamophobia—fear of marriage
10. Thanaphobia—fear of death

One survey suggests that fear of speaking in public, a form of lalophobia, is the most common American phobia. Perhaps two of the less-prevalent irrational fears would be ballistophobia, fear of missiles, and chionophobia, fear of snow. Another fear, one shared by Napoleon Bonaparte and U. S. presidents Herbert Hoover and Calvin Coolidge, is triskaidekaphobia—fear of the number 13.

Perhaps Franklin D. Roosevelt forgot that he too was a victim of triskaidekaphobia when he said, "We have nothing to fear but fear itself."

Bridge

SAY: Humans have little trouble finding something to fear. The intensity of fear or anxiety, of course, varies with the perceived threat to our well-being. In a moment, we're going to look at one remedy for fear. But first, let's check some of our reactions to it.

Activity: *Degrees of Dis-ease*

Have group members line up shoulder to shoulder. Read the first situation described below. Ask the participants to step *forward* one, two, or three paces, depending on the degree of fearfulness they believe the situation would produce in them (three paces being the most fear-producing). If the situation would produce little or no fear or anxiety, have them step *backward* one, two, or three paces (three paces being the least anxiety-producing). Discuss the responses.

1. The Emergency Broadcast System tone (which signifies a threat of potential disaster in one's area) comes on the radio with no warning or explanation.
2. You have been asked to be the main speaker for a school assembly.
3. An escape has occurred at the nearby state penitentiary. At 11:00 that night you hear what sounds like someone tampering with the lock on the back door of your home.
4. You have learned that your mom and dad are thinking of getting a divorce.
5. The morning news informs your city that a package of Happy-O's breakfast cereal from lot 46345 has been found to contain cyanide. You check the box of Happy-O's from which you have just eaten a bowlful. The numbers match.
6. Your telephone rings at 2:00 a.m.
7. The instructor informs your class that only five out of 70 students received an A on the final exam.
8. Tonight is your first date with someone.
9. The special person in your life has just informed you that he or she has been diagnosed with a terminal illness.
10. You are going about 20 miles an hour over the speed limit. Looking in your rearview mirror, you realize the car you've just passed is an unmarked state patrol vehicle.

The Degrees of Dis-ease experience allows participants to see (literally) that fear is common and that, depending on how the perceived threat is processed by the individual, the same stimuli can affect each person differently.

Biblical Perspective

SAY: Fear may have increased in modern society, but the timeless truth found in God's Word can help to conquer it.

One of the great episodes of anxiety recorded in Scripture is found in Matthew 8:23, 24.

"Then he got into the boat and his disciples followed him. Without warning, a furious storm came up on the lake, so that the waves swept over the boat. But Jesus was sleeping."

The necessary ingredients for fear were present. The disciples were on a sinking ship, and their slumbering Savior seemed unconcerned for their safety—and His! But Jesus' sleep was interrupted by his distraught friends. Let's read on.

"The disciples went and woke him, saying, 'Lord, save us! We're going to drown!' He replied, 'You of little faith, why are you so afraid?' Then he got up and rebuked the winds and the waves, and it was completely calm. The men were amazed and asked, 'What kind of man is this? Even the winds and the waves obey him!' " (verses 25-27).

The Savior had calmed both the sea and the fears of His companions.

Application

SAY: The story of Jesus' calming the storm on Galilee is dramatic. It conveys at least three points that can help ease the sting of fear in our lives.

1. **Christians are not immune to fear.** The fact that the disciples had a relationship with Jesus did not eliminate their fearful feelings. Similarly for us, simply knowing Jesus does not alter our basic human perception of danger. But abiding in Jesus does make a difference in how we process our fear.
2. **Fearlessness is tied to faithfulness.** The faith that conquers fear is the result of a consistent relationship with the One who calmed the sea. Placing our trust in Him helps brings a calm assurance and reminds us that we don't need to face our fears alone.
3. **When properly processed, fear helps us grow personally and spiritually.** Fear can be the prelude to something amazing. By relying on Jesus and facing both rational and irrational fears, our character will mature. Perhaps greatest of all is that by refusing to give in to fear, we're destined to develop the rare trait of courage.

Wrap-up

SAY: It's not God's will that His children live in fear. But in a sin-filled world, even devoted disciples may battle this emotion. The good news is that even though our faith is weak, Jesus is able to calm our waves of fear. His instruments may vary—from the simple encouragement of a friend to professional therapy or appropriate medications. But whatever process heaven brings to us for the conquering of our fears, one fact remains: a friendship with Jesus can bring peace in the midst of our storms.

Discussion Questions

1. Did David feel fear when facing Goliath? Can you recall other godly men and women of the Bible who were afraid? How did they deal with their fear?
2. Explain the differences (if any) between worry, anxiety, and fear.
3. Is fear necessary for human survival? Why or why not? If you believe that it is, why does Scripture encourage us not to be afraid?
4. There is a clinical adage that says face the fear and the fear will disappear. Can you think of any examples from your own experience that prove this is true?
5. A friend confides in you that he or she is afraid to fly. As a Christian, what specific course of action might you recommend?

Suggested Scriptures

Psalm 23:4; Philippians 4:6, 7; 1 John 4:18

Notes

____

____

____

____

____

____

____

____

____

DISCIPLESHIP

2
McSpirituality

PURPOSE

To show that attaining true spirituality requires discipline and commitment.

MATERIALS NEEDED

whiteboard or newsprint, marker
Bible
optional: laptop computer

Introduction

SAY: Modern-day disciples do exist. Each of us can probably think of such a person. Maybe it's a church leader, a teacher, or someone else whose deep spirituality shines so bright that you can see it in them.

Ultimately, the goal of Christianity is holiness, a transforming of the mind and spirit. The process of becoming a spiritual person varies from individual to individual. But the Bible reveals a mind-set to be assumed by all of us who want to become more like Jesus. Let's have some fun discovering what it is.

Activity: *The Same Game*

Whet your audience's appetite for discovering some secret ingredients of spirituality. Read aloud the first grouping listed below. Explain that all of the items (or people, etc.) have something in common. They must guess the common element of all. Use the following groupings or create a different set.

1. Dolly, Mary, Eleanor, Betty, Hilary, Laura (U.S. first ladies)

2. team, meat, tame, mate (words using the same letters)
3. Steve Largent, Jim Bunning, Bill Bradley (professional athletes who later served in the U.S. Congress)
4. kangaroo, pita bread, jeans (things that have pockets)
5. college degree, pickle, adulthood, Olympic medal, relationships (things that require a period of time to attain—in other words, delayed fulfillment)
6. Harry Truman, Gerald Ford, George H.W. Bush (left-handed U.S. presidents)
7. fast-food restaurant, ATM, sod, credit card, microwave oven (things that immediately satisfy, or instant gratification)

To conclude, hold up a Bible and ask the audience to consider (without answering at this point) in which of the final three categories (if any) the Bible (and the way of life to which it points) belongs.

Biblical Perspective

SAY: In the world in which we live our desires can be swiftly satisfied. Even on a leisurely day, we may eat at a fast-food restaurant and pick up pictures from a one-hour photo finisher. Later that evening we can fast-forward a DVD to find out "whodunit" before the bad guy even has a chance to do it!

There is still, however, one thing that requires time, discipline, and commitment: a deeper relationship with Jesus Christ.

In the book *Ordering Your Private World* Gordon MacDonald writes, "If we are ever to develop a spiritual life that gives contentment it will be because we approach spiritual living as a discipline, much as the athlete trains his body for competition.[1]

Do you agree or disagree with this? (Allow time for responses and discussion.)

MacDonald isn't the first to suggest that true spirituality requires consistent training. The apostle Paul's wordbrush paints this picture: "Do you not know that in a race all the runners compete, but only one receives the prize? So run that you may obtain it. Every athlete exercises self-control in all things. They do it to receive a perishable wreath, but we an imperishable" (1 Corinthians 9:24, 25, RSV).

The Christians in Corinth who were reading Paul's letter were familiar with the world of sports. Corinth was the host city for the Isthmian games, a series of athletic events second only to the Olympic games in renown.

In the original language the phrase "running a race" is more fully translated "race course." Paul likely had in mind the track in the Corinthian stadium, whose ruins still stand. As for the "perishable wreath," it was a leafy crown made of Isthmian pine. There were no gold, silver, or bronze medals awarded for the Corinth games, but many athletes gladly gave all they had to receive this pine wreath. The ancient writer Horace indicated that a candidate for these games "must be pure, sober, and enduring." Horace added that they must "obey orders" and "eat sparely and simply and . . . bear effort and fatigue for 10 months before the contest."

Becoming a champion takes time and effort. Likewise, prizewinning faith requires discipline and commitment. A person will never earn salvation by this kind of effort, but the gift of grace will be more deeply realized by consistently striving to glorify its giver. That is the race to be run and, through Him, eventually won.

As Paul's passage implies, there is no shortcut to heaven. In a world of quick burgers, there is no McSpirituality. Similarly, no spiritual steroids can achieve what long-term dedication to spiritual discipline can accomplish. That's why Paul wrote, "Let us run with perseverance the race marked out for us" (Hebrews 12:1). Like a runner who is doing everything they can to win the prize, becoming a more devoted disciple takes time and a commitment to know Jesus Christ better. Let's try to produce some collective insight on the subject of commitment.

Activity: *Ten Commandments of Commitment*

This stimulating activity will help individuals strengthen their life commitments. The specific goal is to encourage commitment to spiritual discipline, but the principles may be applied to achieving any goal.

At random, ask for 10 specific suggestions that are likely to help individuals become more committed. Begin each "commandment" with the phrase "Thou shalt . . ." and use King James-style English to finish the sentence(s). Write the commandments on a whiteboard, newsprint, or laptop computer. If your audience is stymied, use one or more of the following examples to help them understand how to choose a commitment goal and how to phrase their commandment.

1. Thou shalt know specifically that to which thou art committing. (focus)
2. Thou shalt be convinced in thine own mind that thy commitment is worth the price thou wilt be paying. (belief)

3. Thou shalt prioritize thy time to achieve the goal to which thou hast committed. (organization)
4. Thou shalt ask for divine assistance in staying committed. (prayer)
5. Thou shalt make thyself responsible to another for thy commitment. (accountability)
6. Thou shalt on occasion place thyself in a situation in which thy commitment can be strengthened through practice. (practical application)
7. Thou shalt try again when thou failest or falter in thy commitment. (recommitment)
8. Thou shalt seek an audience with those who have demonstrated successful commitment. (counsel)
9. Thou shalt increase or decrease thy commitments as thy lifestyle and priorities permit. (growth)
10. Thou shalt encourage others to experience the joy of commitment. (outreach)

As each commandment is suggested, ask for an illustration of how the particular precept might be used. The leader may wish to have these suggestions printed, then distributed the following week.

Illustration

SAY: In his book *It's Always Too Soon to Quit* Lewis Timberlake tells of a man who made a true commitment.

While attending tiny Campbell College in North Carolina, 23-year-old Orville Peterson worked desperately to win a place on the United States track team. After the first day of the decathlon tryouts, Peterson held a solid eighth place in a field of 50 entrants. However, on the second day of the first event, the 100-meter hurdles, disaster paid a visit. Orville Peterson pulled muscles and ligaments in his left thigh; this rendered him virtually immobile.

No one imagined that he could continue with the kind of excruciating pain he must have been enduring. But they were wrong, because Orville Peterson had come to compete. He first refused to see even a trainer for fear he'd be forced to withdraw from the competition. So Orville continued in the next event, the discus throw. While experiencing agonizing pain in his leg, he managed to throw the heavy discus 137 feet 5 inches. After accomplishing this seemingly impossible feat, he pole-vaulted an amazing 12 feet 5 inches as well as threw the javelin 206 feet 9 inches! But these performances, while good under such circumstances, caused him to drop to fourteenth in the standings. Only one event remained on the second day of the competition—the grueling 1500 meters, four laps of sheer misery for even the most fit and healthy athlete.

The crack of the start gun broke the heavy silence as spectators watched in eager anticipation, wondering how this brave young man could even make it around the first lap. The fact is that the winner crossed the finish line in just under five minutes with the rest of the field close behind him. The track was left empty—except for one lone runner.

Orville Peterson, his left thigh heavily wrapped, had promised himself that he'd complete the decathlon competition—even if he didn't win a place on the American team. In spite of his debilitating injury, he was willing to pay the price to achieve his dream. To do this, Orville had to finish the 1500 meters, even if it meant he would have to limp the whole way . . . and limp he did.

As the crowd began to cheer Peterson on, his fellow competitors lined the sides of the track and shouted support. Then the strains of the theme from *Chariots of Fire* poured out of the public-address loudspeakers, filling the stadium with inspiring music. To Orville, this support was bigger and better and meant more to him than becoming another legendary Olympic runner. It was bigger than signing endorsement contracts for sports equipment or athletic clothing, and better than making public appearances.

As Orville entered the home stretch of his final lap of that painful race and headed for the finish line, the PA announcer quietly read this ancient Greek saying to the listening crowd: "Never ask for victory, ask only for courage. For if you endure the struggle, you bring honor to yourself; but most important, you bring honor to us all."

Peterson's time in the 1500 meters that day was nearly 10 minutes, almost twice as long as the winner's time. He earned no points for his effort and dropped to thirty-second place in the final standings. But he had finished the race. And that is why those who were there will testify that Orville Peterson was the biggest winner of all. [2]

Wrap-up

SAY: Orville Peterson knew the meaning of the words "discipline" and "commitment." He was determined to finish the course he was running. Similarly, we Christians who want to grow in grace must devote time and effort to running the race of discipleship.

Yes, there is a race to be run. And all who commit to finishing it will one day claim a prize greater than earthly life itself—an eternity with the Savior.

Discussion Questions

1. Define spiritual discipline. Give some examples of the form(s) it might take in the Christian life.
2. What are some ingredients of spiritual discipline that are common to each of us?
3. What is the role of grace in our race for holiness?
4. Why does Paul tell us to run with perseverance? How does the phrase relate to the assurance of our salvation?
5. Have several individuals tell about a time that commitment (or lack of it) made a difference in their lives. What one thing did each learn about commitment from their experience?

Suggested Scriptures

Psalm 1:1-3; Matthew 7:24-27; John 15:1-8; Ephesians 6:10-18.

Notes

---

[1] Gordon MacDonald, *Ordering Your Private World* (Nashville: Thomas Nelson, 1984), p. 117.
[2] Adapted from Lewis Timberlake, *It's Always Too Soon to Quit* (Old Tappan, N.J.: Revell, 1988), pp. 45-47.

3
Test of Success

PURPOSE

To understand more fully the dynamics of true success for the Christian.

MATERIALS NEEDED

10 index cards, pencils
whiteboard or newsprint, marker
saucepan or basket
optional: laptop computer

PREPARATION

individually cut letters of the alphabet
index cards for activity *The Wealthy Not-So-Old Politician* (distribute these just before the beginning of the program for participants to complete)

Introduction

SAY: Success. The subject catches our personal and financial interest. And who can blame us? After all, advertisers have made it clear that maximum fulfillment awaits those who achieve success. We're taught to savor its flavor and how to dress to gain its favor. And slowly, almost imperceptibly, success becomes the heady object of our affections. We no longer merely *want* to make it to the top. Instead, we *need* to succeed.

When it comes to those who've made it in the eyes of the world, Scripture has painted some intriguing portraits. Depending on the passage, the Bible affirms both rich and poor alike. Is this some kind of biblical mixed message? Or is it possible there is something waiting to be discov-

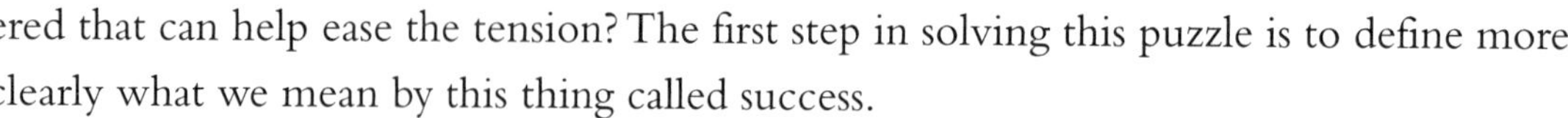

ered that can help ease the tension? The first step in solving this puzzle is to define more clearly what we mean by this thing called success.

Activity: *Success Soup*

Place cut-out letters of the alphabet in a basket or saucepan. (If you have more people than the 26 letters of the alphabet, supply more letters as necessary.) Pass the pan around, and have every group member take one letter. When everyone has a letter, explain that each participant is to think of an attribute necessary for success that begins with their chosen letter. For example, the letter D might suggest the word "dedication." Allow a moment or two for them to think about it, then start around the room, asking each person to share their response. These are written on the whiteboard or newsprint. Do not embarrass anyone who is unable to supply a word. Instead, ask for the group to assist. Also, allow words that begin with a similar sound, such as "excellence" for the letter X.

Success Soup furnishes specific, helpful information concerning what it takes to be a success. It also serves as a lead-in to the next program segment.

Bridge

SAY: The recipe for success contains many ingredients. But minus a Christian framework, our striving for success will ultimately end in failure. Jesus made this very clear in an encounter He had 2,000 years ago. Hopefully, it will come into even greater focus today and help us discover the secret of true success. The names and places may have changed, but the message remains the same.

Activity: *The Wealthy Not-So-Old Politician*

Ask for up to 10 volunteers willing to serve as subjects in a good-spirited experiment that will present a scriptural perspective on priorities and eternal success. Give each volunteer one of the 10 index cards you've previously prepared. Cards should be numbered from 1 to 10, with the instructions as given below.

1. Please write the name of a nearby town:
2. Please write your first name:
3. Please write the name of a local fast-food restaurant:

4. Please write the name of a local discount store:
5. Please write your occupation:
6. Please write a first name other than your own:
7. Please write another first name other than your own:
8. Please write the kind of car you drive:
9. Please write your last name:
10. Please write the name of another nearby town:

Ask the volunteers to fill in the blank on their card. Collect the cards, arranging them in numerical order. Finally, read aloud the story below, inserting the response contained on the index card that corresponds with the number in the script.

Story: *The Wealthy Not-So-Old Politician*

READ ALOUD:

Once upon a time, in the not-so-faraway city of [1] there lived a wealthy not-so-old politician named [2]. Now [2's] life was filled to overflowing with the material benefits his/her station in life afforded him/her. Any evening, on a mere whim, dinner would be catered by [3]. The latest sound system from [4] was just another symbol of the status he/she had attained.

Concerning the specifics of his/her political office, [2] held the powerful position of [5] for the bustling metropolis of [1]. As such, there was little that [2's] occupation could not provide.

Ironically, however, a feeling of discontentment haunted [2]. It was as if, somewhere in the hidden recesses of his/her mind, [2] knew that the ultimate success was yet to appear. Defining the elusive entity, along with a plan for seizing it, continued to evade the savvy and prowess of [2's] otherwise astoundingly brilliant mind.

One morning, as [2] sat reading the [1] *Times*, his/her cell phone rang. It was [2's] personal advisor.

"Did you happen to catch the ad on page 7 of today's [1] *Times*?" [6] inquired. "It appears that yet another scam has found its way to our fair district."

Suddenly very curious, [2] quickly flipped through the pages and found the ad. It read, "Sign Up Now for the Ultimate Success Seminar Sponsored by Eternal Returns, Inc. To register, call 1-800-FOR LIFE."

"So, would you like me to pursue an investigation?" [6] asked shortly.

[2] paused, but finally replied, "Uh, no. I'll check into this myself." With that, the wealthy not-so-old politician hung up and then quickly dialed the number featured in the ad.

A pleasant voice came on the line: "Hello, my name is [7]. Thank you for calling the Ultimate Success Seminar number. Would you like to register now?"

"Yes, I would," [2] replied. This was not to be an undercover maneuver aimed at exposing a potential con game. Rather, the wealthy not-so-old politician hoped to discover the missing link in his/her chain of achievement. So the following Tuesday night [2] pulled up to the seminar site in his/her [8] limousine, stepped out, and walked into the lobby of the [9] Hotel and Convention Center.

[2] had a plan. The Ultimate Success Seminar was scheduled to meet over a period of several weeks. But the wealthy not-so-old politician was a busy person and could not afford to wait that long. After the evening's presentation, he/she would personally approach the presenter. If he were truly a master teacher, as the ad suggested, surely he could quickly furnish the information [2] needed.

The instructor proved to be persuasive yet gentle. It was obvious that he believed deeply in what he was saying. All told, by the end of the evening [2] was convinced that this teacher did indeed have something valuable to offer in unlocking the door to ultimate success. But winners need specific advice from their coach. Accordingly, [2] inched toward the lectern, cleared his/her throat, then spoke. "My good man," [2] began, assuming an air of confidence. "While your stories are captivating, I have further questions."

The teacher's gaze fell on his student, signaling that he had gained his/her mentor's full attention. The wealthy not-so-old politician got to the point. "What I would like to know is what I must do to attain the ultimate success."

The teacher, apparently sensing the status of his questioner, replied, "Surely you already know the 10 basic rules of success. Fact is," he added, pointing to the book that [2] held, "you'll find them in the first portion of your training manual."

"These rules," [2] responded, holding up the manual, "are ancient history. Why, I've been following them since my days back at [10] middle school. So, how about it? What's the real kicker to the big time?"

The teacher paused. He then spoke in caring yet convicting tones. "You lack one thing," he said. "Go," he said. "Forfeit your power and prestige. Then come, and follow me."

A shocked look on [2's] face soon turned to disappointment. The teacher watched with hurt in his eyes as the wealthy not-so-old politician silently walked away. Several associate instructors now gathered around the teacher, apparently awaiting a response regarding the incident. It soon came.

"How hard it will be for those who are driven by achievement to pass the test of ultimate success." Then, turning to his colleagues, he finished by saying, "For many that are first will be last; and many that 'fail' will succeed."

Biblical Perspective

SAY: By now it should be clear that the preceding tale is based on the biblical story of the rich young ruler. While the real rich young ruler asked how to gain eternal life, the story also reveals the principles of true success.

The story of the rich young ruler is found in the tenth chapter of Mark. Here was a man who apparently had it all: wealth, power, prestige, and an ethical record that neared perfection. Here was success personified.

Jesus' eyes, as usual, were not fixed on the outward appearance, but rather on this man's heart. Beginning with Mark 10:17, we see the Master purposefully leading the rich young ruler to a point of spiritual discomfort:

"As Jesus started on his way, a man ran up to him and fell on his knees before him. 'Good teacher,' he asked, 'what must I do to inherit eternal life?'

" 'Why do you call me good?' Jesus answered. 'No one is good—except God alone. You know the commandments: "Do not murder, do not commit adultery, do not steal, do not give false testimony, do not defraud, honor your father and mother." '

" 'Teacher,' he declared, 'all these things I have kept since I was a boy.'

"Jesus looked at him and loved him. 'One thing you lack,' he said. 'Go, sell everything you have and give to the poor, and you will have treasure in heaven. Then come, follow me.'

"At this the man's face fell. He went away sad, because he had great wealth" (verses 17-22).

Ancient ruler or modern disciple—this story contains not only the secret of salvation, but also the answer for all of us who would pass the test of true success. Its discovery is worth our pursuing.

Activity/Discussion

Divide the participants into four groups. Each group is to briefly discuss the following question: What was missing in the "life notes" of the rich young ruler that caused him to fail his test of success? Suggest that reading the remainder of the biblical passage (verses 23-31) may prove helpful.

After a few minutes, have each group reduce their conclusion to 10 words or less. Ask each group to tell their findings aloud, and list these responses on the whiteboard or newsprint. Then ask these questions about the responses:

For the Christian, can these things and the pursuit of earthly success coexist in good conscience?

If not, why not?

If so, how? Ask for specific examples.

Wrap-up

SAY: For a Christian, true success demands a radical, Spirit-driven reorientation. Now, what does that mean? (Give a moment for someone to reply.)

It means that we focus on things of eternity instead of things of earth. And one way to do that is to go after *excellence* instead of *success*.

An author, Jon Johnston, has written about this. He contrasts excellence and success like this. (Read aloud two or three of the seven statements given below. Choose ones best suited for your group.)

Success offers a hoped-for goal. Excellence provides a striven-for standard.

Success bases our worth on a comparison to others. Excellence gauges our value by measuring us against our own potential.

Success grants its rewards to the few, but is the dream of multitudes. Excellence is available to all living beings, but is accepted by the special few.

Success focuses its attention on the external—becoming the tastemaker for the insatiable appetites of the conspicuous consumer.

Excellence beams its spotlight on the internal spirit—becoming the quiet, but pervasive, conscience of the conscientious who yearn for integrity.

Excellence cultivates principles and consistency that ensure that we will treat all persons as intrinsically valuable ends—the apex of our heavenly Father's creation.*

For the Christian, success means living your life on earth as if you were a citizen of the kingdom of heaven. This is an excellent—indeed, the only—way to pass eternity's test of success.

Discussion Questions

1. Is the pursuit of success ever a viable option for the Christian? If so, under what circumstances?
2. Proverbs 16:3 tells us, "Commit to the Lord whatever you do, and your plans will succeed." What does this mean?
3. What are some reasons an individual may grow to love success?
4. How can the Christian know that their priorities regarding achievement reflect God's will?
5. Winston Churchill once said: "Success is not final, failure is not fatal: it is the courage to continue that counts." As a Christian, do you agree or disagree with this statement? What else counts?

Suggested Scriptures

Proverbs 16:3; Matthew 6:19-21; Mark 8:36; Hebrews 12:1, 2.

Notes

---

* Jon Johnston, *Christian Excellence: Alternative to Success* (Grand Rapids: Baker Book House, 1985), p. 33.

SELF-ESTEEM

4
Reflections of the Divine

PURPOSE
To affirm the intrinsic worth of each individual as an image-bearer of God.

MATERIALS NEEDED
paper, pencils for all
whiteboard or newsprint, marker

PREPARATION
none

Introduction

SAY: In the world of collectibles, two of the factors that determine something's value are scarcity and demand. Antique furniture, wind-up toys, a 1955 Ford Thunderbird—plenty of items from the past have become objects of great value.

Wouldn't it be great to own something like that? But what you may not realize is that you already possess something worth more than all of those things combined—your own unique personhood. As to our rarity, each of us is one of a kind. And demand? Christ willingly gave His very life so that He might claim us for His own.

So many of us go through life unaware of our real value, convinced that we are worthless. If only we could realize our true worth as a child of God, our lives would be favorably changed forever.

Low self-esteem is devastating to the person who has it and often to the people around them. When you think—either consciously or subconsciously—that you're worthless, your natural reaction is self-contempt! After all, no one likes a loser. And so *self*—that's who you are—becomes something either to be changed or to be avoided. This may take the form of alcohol or drug abuse, extensive cosmetic surgery, or just staying so busy that one never has to face who they truly are. Tragically, for the most desperate, the solution to self-hatred is suicide.

It's a curious fact that people who think very little of themselves can come across as having a big ego or, by going to the other extreme, as the class clown. Happily, Christians have a real advantage in developing good self-esteem. Yet even Christians encounter barriers to self-worth.

Bridge

SAY: In his book *You're Someone Special*, Bruce Narramore describes an activity that he uses in self-esteem seminars. Borrowing his concept may help us begin to expose some barriers to self-esteem.

Activity: *Pictures of Humility*

Distribute pencil and paper to all participants. Ask them to think of the most humble person they've ever met and then to write down the person's name.

Next, they should write the two words that best describe that person.

When each one has finished, ask class members to read aloud their nomination and the two words they've chosen to describe that individual. Write the two words on the whiteboard or newsprint.

Typically, most of the words in the resulting compilation will conjure up images of exceeding mild-manneredness, such as "quiet" and "reserved." What is usually glaringly absent are words that describe an outgoing and assertive personality style, such as "dynamic" or "enthusiastic."

The purpose of *Pictures of Humility* is to demonstrate the prevailing attitude of viewing humility as a lackluster trait and, concurrently, how that view affects self-esteem.

Application

SAY: As we've seen, the term *humility* evokes a rather specific image in our minds. But as a man named Bruce Narramore writes: "Humility is not passivity. The truly humble person is confident of both his strengths and his rights. With his strength, he can choose to take a position of service or suffering, if that is called for. Because of his inner strength, he can also rise up and aggressively combat evil when circumstances call for action."*

True humility is not merely assuming a lowly attitude. Rather, it is acknowledging dependency on God, regardless of our personality traits.

It's true that Christians are called to use their time and their money wisely. Some people interpret this as living a life of self-suppression. Some think that they cannot have true humility if they recognize the positive things about themselves. The sad result of this skewed view is that the very environment in which self-esteem might grow becomes a desert of unnecessary self-denial. It's only by understanding what true humility is (and is not) that we can build a proper sense of self-worth.

A misconception of humility is one blockade to building self-esteem. But there are many other deterrents on the road to achieving a sense of self-worth. Here are a few. (Write the list on whiteboard or newsprint as you explain each one.)

Negative parental feedback

For many of us the most important element in the formation of our self-worth is the picture we were given by our parents. If yours was a positive experience, you have a greater chance of feeling good about yourself in later life. But if it was negative, your self-esteem probably suffered.

As either parents or persons who may be a child's significant other, it's important for us to be aware of how we might be subtly undermining that child's self-esteem. Some of these ways include:

1. **Conditional love**. Some parents act as if their love for their child depends on performance or a set of rules and conditions. The child learns that outside such circumstances he is unloved. It's hard to love one's self unconditionally when the concept is foreign to one's home experiences.
2. **"Discounting."** Similar to conditional love, this is the conscious or subconscious practice of never giving total affirmation. If the recital piece was 99 percent perfect, Mom or Dad may at first laud the effort but eventually will get around to mentioning the 1 percent imperfection. After a childhood filled with such discounts, it's easy to see how a general sense of inadequacy would develop.
3. **Unempathic bonding**. Some individuals have a bent toward not expressing emotion. Males in particular seem to have a difficult time showing affection. A child is not overtly taught that he is not cared about by the withholding of affection, but the message is inevitably caught. Again, the negative effects on self-esteem can last a lifetime.

4. **Separation and/or divorce.** Psychologists tell us that children tend to assume responsibility for their parent's marital conflicts. "If only I had been a better child, Mom and Dad would still be together" is their unconscious line of reasoning. Obviously a child cannot love themselves if they feel they are to blame for their parents' pain.

Peer rejection

Another key ingredient in forming self-esteem is the way we're treated by our peers. Short neck, long legs, high forehead, low IQ—all can become targets of ridicule. Ironically, those who belittle others usually have a poor self-image themselves. However, "significant others" can counterattack by furnishing massive doses of unconditional love to those so unkindly treated.

Perfectionism

Some people continually set unrealistic goals for themselves. Naturally, when the goals aren't reached, they feel like failures. Such people are trapped on a no-win treadmill. And under these kind of circumstances there is little place for self-esteem.

A key solution is to realize where the pressure is really coming from—from themselves—then either modify what was an impossible goal or grant permission to others to help share the load.

Guilt

Still another barrier to achieving self-esteem is guilt—whether it's false or genuine. Often, when people deliberately focus on guilt feelings, it's because they are subconsciously punishing themselves. Forgiveness just doesn't seem to fit the crime. Accordingly, feeling good about oneself is simply not allowed. Remembering the grace of God is key to setting the guilt-ridden person free.

Excessive competitiveness

A final stumbling block on the road to self-worth is an exaggerated sense of competition. In any contest, if someone wins, another must lose; if there is a first, there is also a last. This arrangement works wonders for those who come out on top. But for the person on the bottom self-esteem can take a beating.

For better or for worse, competition is here to stay. Fortunately, so is God's church. And there's no better place to affirm each other on the basis of who you *are* rather than what you did during the week.

(At this point, solicit from the audience other barriers to self-esteem.)

We've mentioned a few of the many ways in our sin-filled world that a person's self-esteem can be hindered from growing. Psychologists and others could undoubtedly supply more. But Scripture contains an incredible, undeniable fact that can help turn even the poorest self-image around.

Biblical Perspective

SAY: A person's self-worth is rooted in creation itself. Reaching the end of that first week of human history, God capped it off by creating humanity. But perhaps the most amazing fact of this creative act is that God patterned humans after divinity itself! In Genesis 1:26 and 27 we read, "Then God said, 'Let us make man in our image, in our likeness.' So God created man in his own image, in the image of God he created him; male and female he created them."

We are designed as a reflection of the divine! Certainly we are not like God in every aspect, yet we must not deny our heavenly heritage.

Nothing can destroy the reality of our inherent self-worth. It's true that some individuals will not be able to make that truth their own. They'll need the help of the Holy Spirit. And sometimes the Spirit will use you or me as His assistant in the healing process. But healing can happen. The key is realizing that every human being bears this mark of heavenly excellence: *Made in God's image.*

Scripture contains other reasons we can feel good about ourselves. Jesus said we are to love others "as ourselves." Christians in particular can rejoice that they are now heirs of the King of the universe. Finally, as we mentioned earlier, Jesus' death for you and me leaves no doubt as to how much He feels we're worth. According to 1 John 4:19, "we love because he first loved us."

Not only can we can apply this passage to those around us. We can also apply it to ourselves!

Bridge

SAY: As we've seen, Christians in particular have ample reason to harbor a sense of self-worth: we are created in God's image. But we can help others feel good about themselves in a very practical way—by affirming one another. That's something we're going to do right now.

Activity: *Affirmation Diads*

Have the group divide into pairs. One person in each pair is given a minute and a half to tell the listening partner of an achievement, talent, trait, or other source of their own personal pride. The partners then reverse roles, and another 90 seconds is given for the other person to talk. Finally, participants are asked to tell the group about their partners' accomplishments. A lighthearted addition (particularly in a small group format) is to applaud following each presentation.

Affirmation Diads is a simple, effective way to show affirmation for another while affording that individual the experience of being publicly praised.

Wrap-up

SAY: Here's what one Web site said about the "worth" of a human being. "When we total the monetary value of the elements in our bodies and the value of the average person's skin, we arrive at a net worth of $4.50. This value is, however, subject to change, due to stock market fluctuations."

But God's crowning result of creation—you and I—are priceless in His eyes. We're worth more than any amount of money, for the substance of our souls cannot be purchased. We are God's children, made in his image. We are reflections of the divine.

Discussion Questions

1. Are there any scriptural indications of self-esteem in the life of Jesus? (Give examples.)
2. Is the development of self-esteem primarily our responsibility, or is it God's? Explain.
3. What are some specific things we can do to develop self-esteem?
4. The apostle Paul speaks often of the need to deny self. What does he mean by that?

5. Give at least five reasons a healthy sense of self-esteem is important. (List on whiteboard.)

Suggested Scriptures

Genesis 1:26, 27; Psalm 8:3-6; John 3:16; Romans 5:8; Ephesians 2:4-7.

Notes

---

* Bruce Narramore, *You're Someone Special* (Grand Rapids: Zondervan, 1978), p. 61.

5
Did You Get My Message?

PURPOSE

To demonstrate the need of considering context when interpreting Scripture.

MATERIALS NEEDED

whiteboard or newsprint, marker

PREPARATION

cards for *Mixed Messages* activity

Introduction

SAY: For many individuals, reading the Bible is similar to spinning one's tires on ice—they just don't seem to get anywhere.

Although the reasons for this futility vary, there is one secret to studying the Bible that is often overlooked. It's a tool of biblical interpretation called *contextualization*. Simply stated, it means learning about the original circumstances surrounding a particular portion of Scripture. Who wrote it? Why was it written? and To whom was it directed? are some of the important questions that context helps to answer. Understanding this concept can unlock the treasure chest of God's Word.

Illustration

SAY: You probably see it advertised every Christmas. No, it's not the latest techno-gadget or other toy. It's the classic 1946 movie *It's a Wonderful Life*.

In the movie, actor James Stewart plays businessman George Bailey. The Baileys have a picture-perfect family, but on Christmas Eve George learns that his business is about to go bankrupt. A mean banker shows no mercy, making the situation still more dire. After George tries everything he can think of to save the business, he realizes that it's too late. In desperation he dashes off with the intent to leap from a bridge and end his life. George is saved at the last moment by his guardian angel, Clarence.

Clarence shows George just how much his life means by showing him how life in their town would be without him. George's cheerful little town is dreary and impoverished. Without his gentle influence people are mean to each other, and his own dear family doesn't recognize him. In the end George realizes his true worth and goes back home. There the people he's befriended all his life have gathered to support him, personally and financially. The movie ends with a tear-filled reunion, and what promised to be a Christmas disaster turns into the most wonderful Christmas ever for George Bailey.

It's a Wonderful Life is a movie chock-full of love and the value of friends and family. But its message was interpreted quite differently by some at one point in history.

About the time the movie was released, some individuals were concerned about Communism making inroads into the United States of America. As a result, special efforts were made to ensure that messages celebrating Communism were not being covertly shared through the media with U.S. citizens. This included movies.

The Federal Bureau of Investigation had received word that the movie *It's a Wonderful Life* was really a Communist propaganda movie. Here are a couple of excerpts from an official FBI memo regarding the matter:

"With regard to the picture *It's a Wonderful Life* . . . the film represented rather obvious attempts to discredit bankers. . . . This . . . is a common trick used by Communists."

"In addition . . . this picture deliberately maligned [smeared] the upper class."

Regarding the "mean banker," the FBI memo says this: "[the movie] wouldn't have suffered at all in portraying the banker as a man who was protecting funds put in his care by private individuals and adhering to the rules governing the loan of that money rather than portraying the part as it was shown." As it was shown, of course, the banker looked totally heartless. In the story the banker finds a large sum of money that George had lost and does not tell him that he has it.

Looking back, we now know that the movie was nothing more than a heartwarming Christmas story. But had we lived during the time that Communism was seen as a real threat to U. S. freedom, we might have been more suspicious. Understanding the original time and setting, or context, can make a very big difference. And the same is true of how we understand the Bible. When we study it, are we getting the message God intends, or could we be twisting its meaning?

Let's dig a little deeper and have some fun. We'll see what happens when we look at some Bible passages that seem to disagree with each other.

Activity: *Mixed Messages*

Mixed Messages is a fun activity that both enhances the preceding thoughts and leads into application of the concept of contextualization. The absurd results of the exercise will serve to impress more deeply the need for "rightly dividing the word of truth."

Before the meeting, write each of the following Bible excerpts on individual cards, numbering them as indicated.

1. "I am the Lord" "I will bring upon you sudden terror, wasting diseases and fever that will destroy your sight and drain away your life" (Leviticus 26:1, 16).
   - 1a. "God is love" (1 John 4:16).
2. "To the man who does not work but trusts God . . . his faith is credited as righteousness" (Romans 4:5).
   - 2a. "A person is justified by what he does and not by faith alone" (James 2:24).
3. "The Lord God said, 'It is not good for the man to be alone' " (Genesis 2:18).
   - 3a. "It is good for a man not to marry" (1 Corinthians 7:1).

Distribute the cards at random, one card per person. Ask for card 1 to be read aloud, followed immediately by card 1a. Do the same with the other two sets of cards. The seeming contradiction of the corresponding cards will be readily apparent.

Bridge

SAY: There is no shortage of apparent biblical paradoxes. But rather than attempting to simply expose these seeming contradictions in Scripture, let's try to understand them. One way to help do that is by looking at each passage in its original context. By considering whom the passage was first written to and under what circumstances the message was sent, we can usually determine its original intent and better understand how it applies to us today. Let's try it!

Application

SAY: The first passage in the *Mixed Messages* exercise seems to paint a portrait of a God who enjoys distributing pain through terror, sickness, blindness, and death. But can this be the same God who is also defined as love itself? A look at the context of both passages clears up the problem.

The wrathful picture of God's personhood is taken from the twenty-sixth chapter of Leviticus. The writer, whom many believe to be Moses, was recording God's message to the Israelites of the results of turning away from God and the rewards of serving Him. The stiff-necked chosen people badly needed this critical concept driven home—that it is only by serving Yahweh that their ultimate destiny would be fulfilled. Apparently the best way to communicate that truth was by showing the consequences of their decision: serve the Lord, and they would get the Promised Land; discard the divine, and they would die.

As for the more mellow passage, "God is love," it's found in the book of 1 John, chapter 4. Here the apostle is writing as a spiritual father to members of the body of Christ. That's why he calls his readers "dear children."

Besides being a general pastoral Epistle, there was another purpose for this letter. Certain false teachings had made their way into the church (see 1 John 2:18, 19), and John was anxious that amid the confusion the basics of the faith not be forgotten. Accordingly, one of the purposes of his little book was to help "foster the fundamentals," as it were. To achieve that end, John reduces the religious experience to its essence and centers much of this book on a three-word theme: God is love.

Outside a logical frame of reference, the two passages seem to present God as being "two-faced." But a look at the context of each one helps clear up the problem.

The mystery of the second set of *Mixed Messages* is also easily solved by viewing them in context. The book of Romans, in which Paul speaks of trusting God for one's righteousness, is primarily a letter of theology. James, however, is more concerned with practical Christianity.

Therefore, as commentator Burton Scott Easton says, he is writing to "men and women desiring to fulfill properly the tasks of daily life." Easton concludes by saying, "Such teaching James gives them, that and no more."* While Paul wants no mistake made as to the source or root of salvation, James points out that works, or "deeds," are the fruit of true conversion. By understanding the context, both views make sense.

The *Mixed Messages* having to do with marriage are also easier to understand when seen in their original settings. It's clear that marriage is a God-ordained institution. After all, it was our Creator-God who said that it was "not good for the man to be alone." But a closer look at 1 Corinthians 7:l shows that Paul was responding to a specific question, for he begins his counsel by saying, "Now for the matters you wrote about" (1 Corinthians 7:l). He suggests that apparently for some, singleness was a good thing. But interestingly, immediately following is a section of practical advice written for husbands and wives. Clearly, marriage was also still a godly option!

Bridge

SAY: The problem areas of Scripture, such as apparent contradictions, can often be cleared up by understanding their context. Bible dictionaries, commentaries, and other reference tools can help shed light on some of the puzzling areas. Reading a few verses that precede and that follow that problem passage can also help.

But as Timothy wrote, "all Scripture is God-breathed" (2 Timothy 3:16). As such, it transcends human understanding.

It is true that much of the Bible was written for a specific audience. But because Scripture is divinely inspired, these passages contain eternal principles that today's Christian can apply.

Application

SAY: Here are a few suggestions to help us get to the "principle of the thing."

First, having studied its original context, determine what need in today's world the counsel or topic discussed might address. Sometimes this will be obvious, but often a degree of thought and discussion with mature Christians is necessary.

Next, check these conclusions against other portions of Scripture on the same or a related topic. Do they point in the same direction? Other proven works of faith such as classic Christian literature and reference tools may also shed light.

Finally, decide in what practical way this principle might apply to your life. Then do it! Spiritual maturity is demonstrated by living out what you have learned.

Activity: *Principles in Practice*

Using the above concepts, randomly solicit from the group principles drawn either from the texts used in the *Mixed Messages* activity or from other "problem" passages, such as Deuteronomy 7:1, 2; Matthew 5:38-42; 1 Corinthians 14:34, 35; Galatians 3:28.

Write the texts on a whiteboard or newsprint, allowing time for appropriate discussion. Be sure to ask the group to give scriptural support for their ideas. Of course, it is possible that no principle is readily discernible, but encourage the group to consider why such a passage may have been included in the Bible. Finally, ask for a specific example of how each principle might be applied to their own lives.

Wrap-up

SAY: Deciphering the Bible can be a challenge. While many things can help solve its mysteries, looking at the context of a passage is a good place to start. The unintended "Communist message" that some saw in *It's a Wonderful Life* led to a wrong conclusion. We should be sure that our Bible study does not lead us to wrong spiritual conclusions. Through prayer, ask God to assist you in the process of understanding His Word. Handling the Bible properly will bring us closer to leading a wonderful *spiritual* life.

Discussion Questions

1. Is interpreting the Bible ultimately a subjective or an objective matter? Explain.
2. Besides context, what are some other important things to consider when interpreting Scripture?
3. The Bible contains passages that are particularly difficult to interpret. What are some reasons for this?
4. It's possible to lift Bible verses from their context to lend support to something a person wants to do. Can you give any examples of this?
5. Some people believe that God told the Bible writers exactly what to write. Is this a sound theory of inspiration? What are some other ways to look at inspiration?

Suggested Scriptures

Psalm 119:105; 2 Timothy 2:15; 3:15-17; 2 Peter 3:15, 16.

Notes

* *The Interpreter's Bible* (New York, Abingdon Press, 1957), Vol. XII, p. 40.

FRIENDSHIP

6
Friendly Advice

PURPOSE

To affirm the need for meaningful Christian relationships, and explore the dynamics involved in establishing and maintaining them.

MATERIALS NEEDED

whiteboard or newsprint, marker

PREPARATION

Make four photocopies of the script *Dave's Date With Danger* (see p. 46). Assign the various parts prior to the meeting. The drama will be presented in "readers' theater" style.

Introduction

SAY: Everyone needs a friend. But it can be difficult to establish a meaningful friendship. Today's busy world often leaves little time for sharing our hurts and hopes with another. Nevertheless, our need for intimacy at varying levels still exists.

Where does a person turn to find friendship? A sorority house? A nightclub? The Elks' Lodge? In one TV series, *Cheers*, a bar became the spot where at least some level of friendship and camaraderie could be found.

Yet hidden between the scriptwriters' lines resides a serious truth—everybody needs a friend. Everyone needs someone with whom to share laughter and love, triumph, and tragedy.

Bridge

SAY: For many people childhood conjures up thoughts of friendship. The reasons for this may vary. Perhaps there was more to share, maybe less to hide. Whatever the reasons, looking to the past can help us recapture some important elements of friendship.

Activity: *Cherished Friends of Childhood*

Have each person in the group share a childhood experience of friendship (positive or negative). Encourage participants to include names, places, and other details whenever possible and appropriate. This will reveal intriguing and meaningful aspects of group members' past experiences while focusing on friendship.

Bridge

SAY: Sharing memories of childhood relationships is a valuable experience. Too often the feelings surrounding our earlier experiences are forgotten. But there is one thing that looking to the past cannot do. It cannot satisfy today's longing for meaningful friendships.

Although some people opt for a solitary life, we were designed as social creatures. As Jerry and Mary White have written in their book *Friends and Friendship*: "No one can have a meaningful existence without love and friendship. They are the substance of our emotional life." *

(Optional: Ask participants if they agree or disagree with the authors' assertion.)

There's no question that loneliness is alive and well. Yet if friendship is in such high demand, why are so many lives lived out alone?

One possible answer is that many individuals simply don't know how to find a friend. These same people may suffer from the delusion that quality relationships just evolve—that this elusive thing we call chemistry is the ultimate criteria for making friends. But the science of friendship goes much deeper.

While the Bible is first a revelation of how God relates to His children, it also contains helpful insight concerning human relationships. Perhaps no finer example of friendship exists than the story of David and Jonathan. A closer look at their relationship will help reveal some of the secrets of lasting friendship.

Activity: *Dave's Date With Danger*

Use the script beginning on page 46 to tell the story of David and Jonathan's friendship.

Have the preselected participants (those who previously were given scripts and assigned parts) come forward and present this drama in readers' theater style. (Readers' theater is simply a group dramatic reading. Depending on your knowledge of the group, you may also distribute scripts on the spot and just go for it.) The script is taken from the twentieth chapter of 1 Samuel (NEB). Encourage the readers (including the narrator, who fills in between the dialogue) to use the appropriate inflections. Physical actions are unnecessary, although an uninhibited cast might find this a colorful addition.

Ask the audience to note specific characteristics of David and Jonathan's friendship that surface during the narrative. These notes will be used immediately following the presentation.

Bridge

SAY: Many important elements of lasting friendship are found throughout the Bible story of David and Jonathan. A look at some of the traits of their friendship can help us strengthen our own relationships.

Interaction

Following the presentation of *Dave's Date With Danger,* randomly solicit from the audience different attributes of friendship gleaned from the story. Write these qualities in a column on the whiteboard or newsprint, labeling it "Attributes." Next, ask group members to submit words that describe traits opposite of those just mentioned. Write these in a column that corresponds to the previous one, calling this list "Obstacles" (to friendship). Finally, have the audience supply traits for both columns based on their personal observations of friendship—factors that may not have been apparent in this particular narrative. Use the following starters as necessary to facilitate the activity.

Attributes	**Obstacles**
Loyalty	Disloyalty
Transparency	Concealment
Devotion	Apathy
Willingness to defend	Passivity

Intimacy	Aloofness
Trustworthiness	Undependability
Other-centeredness	Self-centeredness
Listening skills	Disinterest/disattachment
Affirmation	Belittlement/discounting

Conclude the experiment by suggesting that when it comes to friendship, the first column (along with the personal observation attributes) contains qualities to be cultivated, while the latter column depicts traits to be eradicated.

Application

SAY: When you nurture positive traits of friendship it can help you establish rich relationships. But along with such specific qualities, there are also some broad principles of friendship that can facilitate the process of finding and keeping good friends:

1. Know what kind of friend you need.

Are you looking for a fellow computer gamer or a prayer partner?

Do you need someone to disciple you?

Perhaps you're hoping to form a new friendship based on what you can offer the other person. That's an excellent approach. Whatever your case, deciding on your goal for a desired relationship will help give you focus as you seek new friends. Of course, just because someone doesn't feel compelled to spend time with you in one area doesn't mean you can't have a close friendship with that person in another area. Be open to all possibilities. Friendship is a valuable commodity.

2. Pace your companionship.

Let friendship develop slowly. Moving in too quickly often quenches what might have become a meaningful friendship. The roots of camaraderie take hold before the fruit of friendship can be picked. Give the plant time to grow.

3. Act on your friendly intentions.

Wishing will never net a friendship; you have got to go out fishing. Avoid the stress of wondering if the other person will take the first step. Instead, take it yourself. You have nothing to lose except your loneliness.

4. Process rejection appropriately.

Not every attempt at friendship is destined to succeed. Understand that, and realize that rejection is more often the result of poor dynamics than a personal affront against you. Let this one go, but don't kick your self-concept around the block and withdraw. Instead, learn what didn't work and apply the knowledge as you reach out again. Someone needs you.

5. Pursue faith-filled friendships first.

It is said that Jesus was a friend of sinners. But it is significant that He chose to share himself in a deeper way with a select few—specifically His 12 disciples and certain other God-fearing individuals. In the tradition of Jesus, today's Christian is called to minister to people across life's spectrum. But it is appropriate that the circle of friendship begin with Christian believers. Branch out from there, always staying rooted in the true Vine.

Wrap-up

SAY: Good friends are a God-sent sweetener of life, and they give life a richness of which too few of us partake. But those who have savored the flavor of a special friendship know that it is a delicacy they cannot do without. Perhaps the time has come for you to experience this delectable fruit called friendship!

NOTE: An effective addition to the wrap-up is to play the song "Circle of Friends," by Point of Grace.

Dave's Date With Danger

Script is adapted from 1 Samuel 20, New English Bible

Characters:

David
Jonathan
Saul
Narrator

Production Notes:

Dave's Date With Danger is designed to be presented in the style of "reader's theater." Readers stand facing the audience; a semicircle works well. Use dramatic inflections and actions as appropriate. Adding music at just the right points can add a dramatic and pleasing touch to the production.

Narrator: Few things in life threaten some of us more than a loss of power. Such was the possibility facing King Saul. In an effort to retain the throne of Israel, he decided to put to death his potential successor, David, the son of Jesse. Ironically, it was Saul's own son Jonathan who helped David avoid an untimely death. The story of this incredible friendship is found in 1 Samuel 20, where David is desperately seeking an answer from his trusted friend, Jonathan:

David *(pleading)***:** What have I done? What is my offense? What does your father think I have done wrong, that he seeks my life?

Jonathan: God forbid! There is no thought of putting you to death. I am sure my father will not do anything whatsoever without telling me. Why should my father hide such a thing from me? I cannot believe it!

David: I am ready to swear to it. Your father has said to himself, "Jonathan must not know this or he will resent it," because he knows that you have a high regard for me. As the Lord lives, your life upon it, there is only a step between me and death.

Jonathan: What do you want me to do for you?

David *(thoughtfully)***:** Tomorrow is the new moon, and I ought to dine with the king. Let me go and lie hidden in the fields until the third evening. If your father happens to miss me, then say, "David asked me for leave to pay a rapid visit to his home in Bethlehem, for it is the annual sacrifice there for the whole family." If he says, "Well and good," that will be a good sign for me; but if he flies into a rage, you will know that he is set on doing me wrong." *(very seriously)* My lord, keep faith with me. You and I have entered into a solemn agreement before the Lord. Kill me yourself if I am guilty. Why let me fall into your father's hands?

Jonathan *(astonished)***:** God forbid! If I find my father set on doing you wrong, I will tell you.

David: How will you let me know if he answers harshly?

Jonathan *(pausing, then speaking softly)***:** Come with me into the fields.

Narrator: So they went together into the fields, and Jonathan said to David,

Jonathan *(intensely)*: I promise you, David, in the sight of the Lord the God of Israel, this time tomorrow I will sound my father for the third time. If he is well-disposed to you, I will send and let you know. If my father means mischief, the Lord do the same to me and even more, if I do not let you know and get you safely away. The Lord be with you as he has been with my father! I know that as long as I live you will show me faithful friendship, as the Lord requires; and if I should die, you will continue loyal to my family forever. When the Lord rids the earth of all David's enemies, may the Lord call him to account if he and his house are no longer my friends.

Narrator: Jonathan pledged himself afresh to David because of his love for him, for he loved him as himself. Then Jonathan said to David,

Jonathan: Tomorrow is the new moon, and you will be missed when your place is empty. So go down at nightfall for the third time to the place where you hid on the evening of the feast and stay by the mound there. Then I will shoot three arrows toward it, as though I were aiming at a mark. Then I will send my boy to find the arrows. If I say to him, "Look, the arrows are on this side of you, pick them up," then you can come out of hiding. You will be quite safe, I swear it; for there will be nothing amiss. But if I say to the lad, "Look, the arrows are on the other side of you, further on," then the Lord has said that you must go. May the Lord stand witness between us forever to the pledges we have exchanged.

Narrator: So David hid in the fields. The new moon came, the dinner was prepared, and the king sat down to eat. Saul took his customary seat by the wall, and Abner sat beside him. Jonathan, too, was there *(pausing, then speaking slowly)*, but David's place was empty. That day Saul said nothing, for he thought that David was absent by some chance, perhaps because he was ritually unclean. But on the second day, the day after the new moon, David's place was still empty, and Saul said to Jonathan, "Why has not the son of Jesse come to the feast either yesterday or today?"

Jonathan: David asked permission to go to Bethlehem. He said, "Our family is holding a sacrifice in the town, and my brother himself has ordered me to be there. Now, if you have any regard for me, let me slip away to see my brothers." That is why he has not come to dine with the king.

Saul *(angrily)***:** You son of a crooked and unfaithful mother! You have made friends with the son of Jesse only to bring shame on yourself and dishonor on your mother. I see how it will be. As long as Jesse's son remains alive on earth, neither you nor your crown will be safe. Send at once and fetch him. He deserves to die.

Jonathan *(outraged)***:** He deserves to die! Why? What has he done?

Narrator: At that, Saul picked up his spear and threatened to kill Jonathan. Jonathan knew that his father was bent on David's death, and he left the table in a rage. He ate nothing on the second day of the festival, for he was indignant on David's behalf. He was angry because his father had humiliated him.

The next morning Jonathan went out into the fields to meet David, taking a young boy with him. He said to the boy,

Jonathan: Run and find the arrows that I am going to shoot.

Narrator: The boy ran on, and Jonathan shot the arrows over his head. When the boy reached the place where the arrows had fallen, Jonathan called out after him,

Jonathan: Look! The arrows are beyond you. Hurry! No time to lose! Make haste!

Narrator: The boy gathered up the arrows and brought them to his master, but only Jonathan and David knew what this meant. The boy knew nothing. Jonathan handed his weapons to the boy and told him to take them back to the city. When the boy had gone, David got up from behind the mound and humbly bowed three times. Then they kissed one another and shed tears together, until David's grief was even greater than Jonathan's. Jonathan said to David,

Jonathan: Go in safety. We have pledged each other in the name of the Lord, who is witness forever between you and me and between your descendants and mine.

Narrator: David went off at once, while Jonathan returned to the city. Their ways had parted for now, but through friendship they were forever united.

Discussion Questions

1. Some would suggest that men have a more difficult time than women when it comes to sharing from the heart. Do you agree or disagree? If you agree, what do you think are the reasons for this difficulty?
2. What are some non-gender-based reasons certain people have an easier time making friends than do others?
3. Many years ago there was a popular tune titled "Everybody Needs Somebody Sometime." Is this true? Can you think of anyone who has boasted of being self-fulfilled without friends? To the best of your knowledge, did their experience bear out their claim?
4. Is a Christian ever allowed to end a friendship? Why or why not? If so, suggest some circumstances that might allow for this.
5. Do you agree or disagree with the idea that the Christian's most intimate friends should be fellow believers? Why or why not?

Suggested Scriptures

Exodus 33:7-11; Proverbs 17:17; 18:24; John 15:13.

Notes

---

* Jerry and Mary White, *Friends and Friendship: The Secrets of Drawing Closer* (Colorado Springs: NavPress, 1982), p. 10.

SUFFERING

7
A Strong Case for Weakness

PURPOSE

To show how God's sovereignty and creative power brings dignity and purpose to human weakness.

MATERIALS NEEDED

pencils, index cards

PREPARATION

Prepare all cards as indicated in the activity *Healer's Helper Classified Ads.*

Introduction

SAY: At first glance, some things just don't seem to belong together. But a second look often proves otherwise. Take, for example, Milton Hershey's creative candy, bittersweet chocolate. If the stuff is bitter, how can it be sweet? Conversely, if the stuff is sweet, how can it be bitter? Who knows? But it is.

Candy companies are not the only people who have fused seeming opposites. Etymologists have placed words together that logically shouldn't be together. These hybrid phrases are called oxymorons. "Reginald was sadly amused" is a good example of an oxymoron. Even the prolific writer James Thurber used oxymorons His word picture, "a little bit big," seems strange. Apparently, however, in the world of oxymorons all things are possible.

The examples of such self-contradicting combinations could go on. Not that all things that go together but shouldn't are opposites. We may each have our own combination that has worked, but shouldn't have!

Activity: *Oppalikes*

This activity, in a relaxed and potentially humorous way, shows the strange combinations in life that somehow end up working for the individuals involved.

Ask group members to think of an apparently ominous combination in their experience that had a successful outcome. This could be something as simple as a peanut-butter-and-banana sandwich, or as significant as an interracial marriage. Allow a brief time for thinking (background music may be appropriate during this time), then have the participants tell their recollections.

Bridge

SAY: As we have seen, opposites, or at least apparent incongruencies, can often work together. But perhaps nowhere is this truth more evident than in 2 Corinthians 12:10. Let's look at the apostle Paul's weak strongman.

Biblical Perspective

The chapter begins with Paul saying that he knew a man who had been to the "third heaven." Scholars are uncertain what this third heaven actually was, but most of them believe that Paul was talking about himself. But despite this incredible experience, something was allowed to come Paul's way to help keep him humble. Beginning with verse 7 of 2 Corinthians 12 we read:

"To keep me from becoming conceited because of these surpassingly great revelations, there was given me a thorn in my flesh, a messenger of Satan, to torment me. Three times I pleaded with the Lord to take it away from me. But he said to me, 'My grace is sufficient for you, for my power is made perfect in weakness.' "

Paul is convinced that with Christ in control, his struggles can make him stronger. His concluding thoughts on the subject are found beginning with verse 9: "Therefore I will boast all the more gladly about my weaknesses, so that Christ's power may rest on me. That is why, for Christ's sake, I delight in weaknesses, in insults, in hardships, in persecutions, in difficulties." Paul then ends with a paradox: "For when I am weak, then I am strong."

As Paul's list suggests, "thorns" come in many forms. And while times may have changed, strife is still with us. Weaknesses? Even the strongest of us has them. As for insults, no one's skin is thick enough not to have felt their occasional sting. Hardships? The local social services agencies can furnish a long list of those in need. Nor are persecutions a thing of the past. And difficulties? In her book *Choices, Changes*, Joni [pronounced Johnny] Eareckson-Tada, a quadriplegic herself, shares a small sampling of such despair. She has returned to Los Rancho Hospital in southern California, where years earlier she had undergone physical therapy. We find Joni talking with a hospital employee:

"You met the guys in OT?" [Debbie] asks, turning the conversation away from herself.

"Yes." I nod and then add, "Things in occupational therapy haven't changed much . . . potholders and paints and stuff. But those guys seem to have a good attitude about it."

Debbie's smile fades. "Well, not all of them. Did you meet the boy with the halo cast?" I nod again. "His parents don't want anything to do with him. He broke his neck in a motorcycle accident, driving when he was drunk. They figure he got himself into this mess, so he can get himself out." She sighs and shakes her head.

I wince and look toward the window of the therapy room. I wish I had said more to him.

"And the good-looking paraplegic? His wife just filed for divorce. I've tried talking to him about God, but he just won't listen. He's losing himself . . . in pity. In drugs."

I stare at the therapy room windows. The stories she relates are strikingly similar to many I heard when I was at Rancho as a patient years ago. But they didn't touch me then as they do now. *

Thorns. None will escape their pointed pain. But as Joni Eareckson-Tada learned, thorns can either break you down or make you stronger. The secret lies in giving them over to God. By so doing, as Paul discovered, the weight of dependency shifts from self to Jesus. That is the formula for growing in grace.

But there is another positive aspect of being weak in ourselves, yet strong through Jesus Christ. While you may have a personal desire to be healed of a difficulty, or thorn, God may have a grander purpose in mind for your pain. When human thorns are given over to His power, their owners are enabled to become Healer's helpers. That's a way of saying that they are now well qualified to assist the Holy Spirit in the healing of another. Put another way, misery is often the boot camp of ministry. No one can comfort a hurting person better than one who has personally been there. Let's explore just how that can happen.

Activity: *Healer's Helper Classified Ads*

This activity is designed to show how human weaknesses, or "thorns," when given over to God's power and creativity, can become tools for ministry. *Note:* If your audience is primarily high school age, you should write situations that more closely reflect the experiences of their age group.

Divide the audience into four groups. Distribute to each group one 3" x 5" index card with the heading Healing Wanted. Or print these four situations in 3" x 5" boxes to be photocopied and cut. One of the following situations should appear on each card:

1. I am a 19-year-old student attending a state university. Last year I was a consistent weekend party person—a great way to make friends, but a lousy way to live. I made a commitment during the summer to maintain the relationships but to quit doing the stupid things I was doing to myself. Little by little, though, my former friends are leaving me out of their lives. I really need someone to talk to. Can you help?
2. I am a 27-year-old male and an Iraq War veteran. I have a purple heart and a wheelchair to prove it. When I returned from Iraq, my wife seemed willing to accept the paralysis. But something—or more accurately, someone—has changed her mind. She left this morning. I don't know whether it's worth trying to go on. I am desperate for some answers.
3. I am a 31-year-old street person. I have tried many times to kick my booze habit and get on the road to a better life. But sometimes I feel as though I'm destined to die in the gutter. Nobody wants to give guys like me a break—at least not doing something that's legal. Does anybody out there care?
4. I am a single 29-year-old entrepreneur. One year ago I left a position with Tech Systems to start my own business. Unfortunately, my dream is not being realized, and the business is failing. I see filing for bankruptcy as my only option. I have always been plagued by low self-esteem and had hoped that a successful business venture would help. Obviously, the current situation is causing the opposite to happen. I need someone to turn to. If you are qualified to help, please reply soon!

Each ad is to be responded to (by the small group) by supplying a one- or two-paragraph hypothetical, yet realistic, "application for employment." Take note that gaining the position of Healer's helper is based on "redeemed weakness," or "thorns," that have been committed to Christ, not on human skills or strengths. An example response to number 4 might be:

Name: Heather Hansen

Age: 33

Situation Summary: Because of downsizing, Heather was recently let go from her position as administrator with the local Small Business Administration office.

Qualifications for Healer's Helper: As a result of my termination, I have had to overcome the loss and bitterness it brought. Sharing the details of this process with someone in your circumstances could prove helpful to you at this time. In addition, since I now find myself with more free time than in the past, I would be willing to devote some of it to consulting with you regarding alternatives for the future of your business venture.

Allow the groups five to seven minutes to prepare their responses. Encourage the participants to avoid, if possible, simply responding as one whose situation has been identical to that of the advertiser's. Instead, suggest that replies be based on appropriate *principles of healing* drawn from the respondent's hypothetical situation. At the end of the allotted time, have each group tell both their situation and the group's collective response/résumé.

The idea behind this exercise is to portray more than a silver lining approach to problems. It is to help individuals begin to see how God can use one's hurts in the healing process of another. Deepen this concept by pointing out that, while human creativity can discover potential strength in weakness, how much more can God, "who is able to do immeasurably more than all we ask" (Ephesians 3:20), provide opportunities for turning struggles into strengths.

Wrap-up

SAY: Thorns can either destroy us or they can drive us to depend more on God, to be used of Him. From Joseph to Job to the apostle Paul, the Bible tells us that there is purpose in our pain. The weak strongman is no absurdity. It is simply another of God's impossible possibilities. Our weaknesses do become our strengths when the thorns in our lives are taken to the throne of God.

Discussion Questions

1. Besides those already mentioned, what are some biblical examples of individuals using their weakness to glorify God?
2. What are some effective ways to help an apathetic individual become motivated to turn a weakness into a strength?
3. What are some guidelines to follow in deciding if and when others should be told about one's former weakness?

4. Does the experience of having been through a time of difficulty automatically qualify one to be a Healer's helper? Why or why not? If not, what further requirements might be necessary?
5. Who are some Healer's helpers who have made a significant impact upon your own life?

Suggested Scriptures

Book of Job; Romans 8:37; 2 Corinthians 1:3-7, 12:1-10; Philippians 3:7-11; Hebrews 4:15.

Notes

---

* Joni Eareckson-Tada, *Choices, Changes* (Grand Rapids: Zondervan, 1986), p. 35.

RISK

8
Risky Business

PURPOSE

To show that intelligent, redemptive risk adds dimension to life and provides unique opportunities for Christian service and personal growth.

MATERIALS NEEDED

whiteboard or newsprint, marker

PREPARATION

The initials from each name listed in the activity *Chance of a Lifetime* should be written in column form on the whiteboard or newsprint.

OPTIONAL WARM-UP ACTIVITY: REFLECTING ON RISK

At random, ask individuals to tell about one of the following situations: (1) a risk that he/she has gladly taken, (2) a risk taken that he/she regrets, or (3) a risk that he/she would like to take.

Introduction

SAY: In his book *Who Switched the Price Tags?* Tony Campolo documents the results of an intriguing sociological study. Each of the 50 participants was age 95 or older and had been asked to respond to one question: If you could live your life over again, what would you do differently? One of the things consistently reported by many of these old folks was this: If they could do it differently, they would take more risks.[1]

This is worth thinking about. What is risk? One dictionary defines it as "a chance of encountering harm or loss; hazard; danger." If that description is true, we wonder why the surveyed senior citizens wished that they had done it more often!

Obviously, not all risks are a sure thing. If they were, more would undoubtedly be taken. But while the majority of us choose security, there are people who have taken their chances and—for better or worse—reaped the rewards of their risk. Let's consider a few of them.

Activity: *Chance of a Lifetime*

This activity is a form of word association. Call out each name listed below to a different individual in your group. Point out that each one is known to have taken a risk in life. Immediately after hearing the name, the person called is to say aloud the first adjective (a word of description) that he or she associates with that name. The leader (or assistant) then writes that word following the appropriate initials on the board or newsprint (as described in Preparation). Do this for each of the following names:

1. Joan of Arc
2. George W. Bush
3. Christopher Columbus
4. Monica Lewinsky
5. Steve Irwin (aka the Crocodile Hunter)
6. Martin Luther King, Jr.
7. Christa McAuliffe
8. Dr. Jack Kervorkian
9. Mother Teresa
10. Elijah

(Suggestion: Add to or replace with names from current events.)

After all of the words have been recorded, point out the varying responses. While each individual named had taken risks in their life, the words used to describe the person suggests an impression their particular risk made on another (in this case the person responding).

Chance of a Lifetime is designed to show that every risk produced consequences, good or bad.

Bridge

SAY: In and of itself, risk is neither good nor bad. But as the previous experience has shown, risk reaps results. For better or worse, risk changes lives.

It's true that results can sometimes serve as an indicator of a risk's worthiness. But is the end product an accurate barometer of the merit of a given risk? If not, what criteria may be used in deciding whether taking a chance in a given situation is wise? Let's look at a true story that will allow us to grapple with those questions.

Case Study: *Operation Auca*

On January 3, 1956, five men took a risk for God. Feeling led by Him, this quintet of dedicated missionaries had decided to attempt to establish contact with Ecuador's Auca Indians. They were aware that the term *Auca* meant savage in the local dialect. They also knew that the title was well deserved. In 1942 three employees of the Shell Oil Company were killed while prospecting for oil in Auca territory. The following year the number rose to eight. And these were not the first of the Indians' victims. Of the apparent randomness of the Auca slayings, Elisabeth Elliot, wife of one of the five missionaries, wrote: "One fact only seems firmly established: the white man is unwanted. When he sets foot within the area that the Aucas have marked off for themselves, he risks his life."

Nevertheless, the five men had purposed to serve the Lord among the various Indian tribes of Ecuador. Their respective decisions had not been made lightly.

During college Jim Elliot had spent much of a 10-day period in prayer. The issue: whether or not to enter full-time mission service. The answer seemed to be an unequivocal yes.

Pete Fleming was a longtime friend of Elliot's. After grappling with God during his graduate studies, Fleming decided to serve the One whom he had questioned. He wrote his fiancé, "I think a 'call' to the mission field is no different than any other means of guidance. . . . A call is nothing more or less than obedience to the will of God."

Another friend of Jim Elliot's, Ed McCully, was a law student at Marquette University. He had taken a night job as a hotel clerk and would often read his Bible during free moments. Convicted by a passage in Nehemiah, he wrote a letter to Jim Elliot. Part of it read: "I have one desire now—to live a life of reckless abandon for the Lord, putting all my energy and strength into it. Maybe He'll send me someplace where the name of Jesus Christ is unknown." Ed and his wife, Marilou, would one day sense that call.

Nate Saint and his wife, Marj, had come to Ecuadorian Indian territory in 1948. Theirs was an aviation ministry in conjunction with the Missionary Aviation Fellowship. Medicine and other items were more readily available thanks to Nate's little Piper.

In 1953 Roger and Barbara Youderian, along with their 6-month-old daughter Beth Elaine, came to assume duties at the Macuma mission station in Ecuador. Earlier, in a letter to his mother, Roger had written: "Ever since I accepted Christ as my personal Savior last fall . . . I've felt the call to either missionary, social, or ministerial work. . . . Can't say now what the calling will be, but I want to be a witness for Him and live following Him every second of my life." To Roger Youderian, the call to the mission field was confirmed in his soul.

By 1954, both of the bachelors, Jim Elliot and Pete Fleming, had married. All five of the missionary families had now come into contact with each other. One goal was shared by all: to reach out with the gospel to the killer Auca Indians.

There were, however, moments of reticence. Pete wrote, "The thought scares me at times, but I am ready. We have believed God for miracles, and this may include the Aucas. It has got to be by miracles in response to faith. No lesser expedient is a shortcut. O God, guide us!"

On September 19, 1955, Nate Saint and Ed McCully spotted an Auca settlement from the air. It was to be dubbed Terminal City. Months of collective brainstorming and preparation followed that initial sighting. In a gesture of friendliness, gifts and photographs of themselves were dropped from the air. The Aucas responded, eventually tying a return gift on the line dangling from the plane. Ed McCully's diary records the event: Nate made a perfect drop. I held the line and could feel their holding onto it. They cut the pot off—and tied something on! When we got back to Arajuno, we found that it was a llaitu, or headband of woven feathers. A real answer to prayer; another sign to proceed . . ."

After several such signs throughout the next few weeks, the date was set. On January 3, 1956, the plane would set down at Palm Beach, a clearing in Auca territory.

That Tuesday, after landing, the men began setting up camp. Here they would anxiously await the arrival of the Aucas, for to venture unbidden into their village was not an option.

By Thursday evening there had been no contact made by the Indians. But as the sun set Nate Saint wrote, "We find that we have friendlier feelings for these fellows all the time." He then went on: "We must not let that lead us to carelessness."

Friday morning, 11:15. Apparently in response to Ed's calling into the jungle, three

Auca Indians stepped into the open area across the river—one man accompanied by two women. They gestured for someone to come over to their side of the river. Jim Elliot cautiously entered the water. The Indians followed him, and Jim led them back to his own side of the river. By referring to their phrase books, the missionaries were able to convey the idea to the trio that they need not be afraid. The man, whom the five arbitrarily called George, took an interest in the plane. Nate took him up, flying over the Auca village still several miles away. It would be the first of three rides for the native.

That afternoon the trio departed, leaving the five missionaries to rejoice. Eventually Nate and Pete returned to the mission station, while Jim, Ed, and Roger sat out an uneventful Saturday.

Sunday morning, as Nate and Pete climbed into the plane to return to Palm Beach, Pete called out: "So long, girls. Pray. I believe today's the day."

At 12:30 Nate radioed back to base that a "commission of 10" Aucas had been seen making their way toward the camp from Terminal City. "Looks like they'll be here for the early-afternoon service. Pray for us. This is the day! Will contact you next at 4:30."

At 4:30, however, the airways were silent. Throughout the night the radio was monitored, but there was no word from the men.

By 7:00 Monday morning, January 9, a colleague of Nate Saint's, Johnny Keenan, was in the air flying toward Palm Beach. By 9:30 the first report came to Marj Saint. She relayed this message to the other wives: "Johnny has found the plane on the beach. All of the fabric is stripped off. There is no sign of the fellows."

The search continued until on Wednesday, January 11, Johnny Keenan spotted a body floating facedown in the river. A closer look revealed a broken lance protruding from its hip. Around the lance was wrapped a gospel tract.

By Wednesday afternoon the United States Air Force had joined in the search. It was again Johnny Keenan, however, who spotted the second body.

On Thursday two canoes of Indians from another tribe were encountered. One of them, who had been converted to Christ by Ed McCully, informed the search party that they had found Ed's body on the beach.

By Friday, January 13, 1956, the two remaining bodies had been found. The search was over. Five missionaries, certain of their calling to minister among the Auca Indians, had been killed by the ones they longed to serve.[2]

Discussion

Stimulate discussion on wisdom in risk-taking by immediately asking the question, "At the time, was Operation Auca a 'good' risk?" Follow up the comments with this question: Several years after the murder of these five men the first of the Auca Indians submitted his life to Jesus Christ. Since then, many more of the Auca have chosen to follow Him. Does this make a difference in your assessment of the worthiness of the risk taken?

Allow ample time for various responses. While maintaining focus of the issues is necessary during the discussion time, do not force a preconceived opinion. Direct the discussion so that participants consider the dynamics involved in the decision-making process of the five missionaries. This will help foster a productive learning experience, rather than merely casting judgment on the men.

Bridge

SAY: Apparently Nate Saint foresaw the potential for controversy in Operation Auca. Less than a month before his death he wrote, "As we weigh the future and seek the will of God, does it seem right that we should hazard our lives for just a few savages?" He answered affirmatively, reasoning that "it is the simple intimation of the prophetic Word that there shall be some from every tribe in His presence in the last day, and in our hearts we feel that it is pleasing to Him that we should interest ourselves in making an opening into the Aucas' prison for Christ."[3]

As mentioned, through the years many Auca Indians have become Christians through the witness of some of widows of the slain men and of others sharing the gospel with the tribe. That part of Nate Saint's dream came true.

Biblical Perspective

SAY: The Bible shows us some key ingredients in good risk-taking. A look at a few of the biggest risk-takers of Scripture—Abraham, David, Elijah, and others—reveals at least two common factors. First, they had a solid relationship with God. And second, their risks were redemptive at their core. Their gambles were taken with God's purposes in mind. The results were aimed at benefiting something or someone other than themselves.

Few, if any, theories are foolproof. But the theory of redemptive risk works well in many instances.

Are you afraid to risk loving again? Redemptive risk says to look outside yourself and realize that someone else may need your love.

Should you take a chance on the stock market? Redemptive risk says to consider when and where your money can best be used for others. It may be that the stock market would be your best bet. But it could also be that a starving child will survive another day because you gave today.

Whatever the risk you are facing, Scripture has made clear that a redemptive risk, taken in relationship to God, often reaps positive and eternal rewards.

As Abraham left Ur of the Chaldees, as Elijah called down fire from heaven, and as David took on the giant Goliath, each knew that the risk he was taking was designed to reflect the glory of God. Perhaps the risk taken by five missionaries in Ecuador was also made with the same thought in mind. They knew in whom they had believed, and to further His cause was, for them, worth the risk.

Application

SAY: Obviously there is a limit to the energy you can devote to a decision involving risk. But there are some specific actions you can take to help avoid unnecessary agony when facing risk.

1. Ask yourself: Will taking this risk afford me the opportunity to love God, myself, and others better?
2. Count the cost(s), to yourself and others, of a given risk, and weigh them against the potential rewards.
3. Seek the counsel of others with experience, and pray that your ultimate choices and timing will reflect God's sovereign will.
4. When the results of a well-reasoned risk prove negative, reflect on it but do not play it over and over in your mind. Negative thinking will not bring about a positive result.
5. With God as your guide, risk again. When we pursue only that which is certain, we run a still greater risk: a life of mediocrity. Someone has put it this way:

Risks

To laugh is to risk appearing the fool.
To weep is to risk appearing sentimental.

To reach out for another is to risk involvement.

To expose feelings is to risk exposing your true self.

To place your ideas, your dreams before a crowd is to risk their loss.

To love is to risk not being loved in return.

To live is to risk dying.

To hope is to risk despair.

To try is to risk failure.

But risks must be taken because the greatest hazard in life is to risk nothing.

The person who risks nothing does nothing, has nothing, and is nothing. They may avoid suffering and sorrow, but they cannot learn, feel, change, grow, or live. Chained by their certitudes, they are a slave; they have forfeited their freedom.

Only a person who risks is free.

Wrap-up

SAY: Jesus Christ Himself took the biggest redemptive risk of all time, for He had the most to lose—a world dying to sin. Like so many Christians since, the urge to share the good news about God drove Him to take the risk of being rejected. And while He was indeed destined to lose something—His very life—the story would not end there. For God would call Him from the grave, and He would enjoy the reward of His risk—His children—throughout eternity.

Discussion Questions

1. Define "good" risk and "bad" risk.
2. What advantage, if any, does the Christian have in assuming risk?
3. Should Christians always avoid unnecessary risk? Why or why not?
4. What are some biblical examples of taking risks? Was the outcome positive or negative? Why?
5. Business leader Peter Drucker has suggested that there are four types of risks: (1) the risk one must accept, (2) the risk one can afford to take, (3) the risk that one cannot afford to take, and (4) the risk that one cannot afford *not* to take.

Do you think this assessment of risk is correct? What might be an example of each point?

Suggested Scriptures

1 Samuel 17; 1 Kings 18:1-39; Matthew 21:12, 13; Philippians 2:25-30.

Notes

____

[1] Anthony Campolo, *Who Switched the Price Tags?* (Waco, Tex.: Word, 1987), pp. 28, 29.
[2] Elisabeth Elliot, *Through Gates of Splendor* (New York: Harper, 1957). The story is reconstructed from the book.
[3] Ibid., p. 176.

9
The Name Behind the Good News

PURPOSE

To promote a greater understanding of and appreciation for the sacredness of God's name.

MATERIALS NEEDED

3" x 5" index cards, pencils

a book listing names and their meanings (a good resource is an online or printed name dictionary).

PREPARATION

As individuals enter, ask them to write their first name on the index card. Have an assistant look up the meaning of their name in one of the sources mentioned above. Write the name's meaning on the reverse side of the card. (If a name is not listed, and if the person does not know the meaning of his or her name, have them write a definition that includes a distinguishing personality trait.) These will be used in the activity *The Name Game.*

Introduction

SAY: Imagine that you live in a world where names are no longer used. Instead, for efficiency's sake, everything and everyone is assigned a number. For example, certain automobiles, computers, and even an occasional breakfast cereal are identified by a number instead of a name.

Computers love this system, because it's easy to keep things straight. But imagine asking for a date using digits.

"Hello, is this 27496? This is 83224. You don't know me, but you work with my best friend, 44328. He's asked 76581 to go to the symphony next Tuesday night, and he thought maybe you'd be interested in going as my date. You would? Great, 27496! I'll pick you up at 7:00."

Obviously, without a name there's something missing. There's a lack of emotion, a coldness that deadens the sense of anticipation.

A name helps give personal identity to an individual. To enhance this uniqueness, parents often choose a name that reflects some specific meaning. For example, some of the Puritan names from England were very descriptive. Among those found on a 1658 jury roll call were these: The-Gift-of-God Stringer, Joy-From-Above Brown, and Search-the-Scriptures Morton. And once, when a Puritan maiden was asked for her baptismal name, she replied, It's Through-Much-Tribulation-We-Enter-the-Kingdom-of-Heaven, but for short they call me Tribby."

Fascinating. But we need not research published reports of intriguing names, for there are some colorful handles close at hand.

Activity: *The Name Game*

Select one of the name cards participants filled out earlier. Say aloud the *meaning* of the person's name and have the group attempt to guess whose name it describes. Do this for as many individuals as time allows. (Be sensitive to any who may feel self-conscious about their unusual name.)

This activity helps everyone become more familiar with the names of all members while developing the program theme.

Thought Talk

SAY: We've looked at *people's* names, but *products* typically have names as well.

Have you noticed how the brand names of certain products often become household terms? The technical term for this misuse of a trade name is called "eponomy." For example, people seldom make a "photocopy." Rather, when we wish to duplicate an important paper, we make a "Xerox copy" or we say, "I need a Xerox of this."

The brand name Xerox comes from the word "xerography." This is the technical process that takes place in photocopying. Therefore, a true Xerox copy is made only on a machine bearing that name.

Another product name often used without thought is Scotch Tape. In truth, there is just one genuine Scotch brand adhesive tape that is manufactured by the 3M Company.

The story goes that this product gained its name from the fact that originally the adhesive was applied in thin strips only along the edges of the cellulose film. Dissatisfied customers contacted the manufacturer and suggested they not be so "Scotch" (or stingy) with their sticky stuff. The company got the message and called their new version Scotch tape. (Even if the story is an embellishment, it seems to have stuck, although it probably should've been called non-Scotch tape.)

The list of eponomous names could go on: Jacuzzi, Jell-O, Kleenex, and many more. But there's another name that through the years has been more mistreated than perhaps all others combined. It's not the name of a product, but rather the title of the One to whom we pray—God.

Bridge

SAY: Just like the personal names we each have, God's name also has a meaning. But in the same way people thoughtlessly ask for a piece of "Scotch" tape to repair a torn "Xerox" copy, so God's name is often used without thinking.

Scripture contains many different designations for God. As theologian William Dyrness suggests, "God is personal in that He is the God who gives Himself a name."[1] Interestingly, each title for God found in the Bible reflects a certain characteristic about Him and His relationship to His people.

Activity: *Knowing His Name*

Assign the following Bible texts to be read aloud:

1. Genesis 31:53
2. Genesis 17:1
3. Psalm 50:14
4. Genesis 16:13
5. Deuteronomy 32:4
6. Genesis 1:1
7. Psalm 24:7

After each passage is read, briefly explain the meaning of the title for God used within the verse, or invite those in your group to do so. Following are some generally accepted definitions as rendered in the original Hebrew.[2]

1. Genesis 31:53: "the God of Abraham." *El.El.* Some believe this to be the oldest Semitic name for God. It means "mighty leader" or "governor," and stresses the distance between humanity and divinity. *El.El* also speaks of His power over the natural world.
2. Genesis 17:11: "the Almighty God." *El Shaddai.* This title is a compound name using the previous designation, *El*, as a preface to *Shaddai.* The literal translation is unknown, although some scholars believe it could mean "God of the Mountains," referring to the mighty and exalted character of God.
3. Psalm 50:14: "fulfill your vows to the Most High." *Alion.* This name indicates the supreme position of God.
4. Genesis 16:13: "the God who sees me." *El Roeh.* Again, a compound name. As the verse indicates, it refers to God's sovereign "sight," a watching over His earthly children.
5. Deuteronomy 3:24: "Sovereign Lord." *Yahweh.* Here is the name by which the Israelites knew God. It refers to His absolute, unchanging nature, and is connected with the covenant relationship. As such, it embraces the idea of nearness and concern for His chosen people.

   Jewish individuals do not pronounce the name *Yahweh*, as speaking God's name aloud is considered inappropriate. For example, in reading the Scriptures aloud, *Adonai*, a word meaning "the Lord," is substituted for *Yahweh.* The mysterious title God instructed Abraham to refer to him as "I am who I am" (Exodus 3:14), is also associated with the name *Yahweh.*
6. Genesis 1:1: "In the beginning God created." *Elohim.* The name here may be interpreted two different ways. Some scholars feel that it points to the justice of God, while others believe it refers to the majesty of His being.
7. Psalm 24:7: "the King of glory." *Melek.* As the translation indicates, God is also seen as royalty, the one who reigns as king over all.

Ask the group members for other titles or names by which God is called, along with their meanings, if known. Knowing His name provides valuable information on the multidimensional aspects of God's name.

Application

SAY: God is known by many descriptive names in the Bible. But despite the number and variety of His titles, they undoubtedly capture only a small part of His unmatched glory and greatness.

In earlier Bible times, death was the punishment for misusing God's name. It's true that Jesus' death on Calvary gave us a new way of relating to God. Now, a person doesn't go through a system of sacrifices to connect with our heavenly Father—we can approach Him directly. But just because we have a more intimate way of relating to God doesn't mean we can treat His name casually.

Sadly, in today's culture taking God's name in vain has become all too common. Media such as TV and movies try to raise their ratings by writing God's name as a curse word into their scripts. They can be thankful that they're not living in ancient Bible times. As theologian R. C. Sproul wrote, "If Old Testament laws were in effect today, every television network executive would have long ago been executed." [3]

Whatever the rationale underlying the abuse of God's name, spoken or unspoken, one thing is clear: God is not pleased with such profaning of His holiness. This is supported by the third commandment: "You shall not misuse the name of the Lord your God, for the Lord will not hold anyone guiltless who misuses his name" (Exodus 20:7). In God's book, blasphemy is serious business.

What can we do to curb the trend? Here are some suggestions:

1. **Beware the media's message.** There is an advertising adage that says, "Repetition deepens effect." In other words, constant exposure to something, whether good or bad, increasingly embeds its message in our minds.

   If you watch popular TV sitcoms or if you listen to much contemporary music you've probably experienced how often media abuses God's name. Remain sensitive to that fact and communicate your disapproval to those who sponsor it. Otherwise, all this blasphemy will continue to be seen as normal.
2. **Know the character of God.** Through the study of Scripture and other material begin to get a firmer grip on who God really is and what He stands for. A deeper understanding of His divine attributes, particularly holiness, will result in a greater sense of reverence for God's name.
3. **Affirm His holiness within relationships.** Silence can speak loudly when it comes to God's holy name. Refuse to employ the name of God flippantly in casual

conversation. In doing so, you will be quietly allowing others to see that He holds a very special place in your heart.

(If time allows, solicit further suggestions from group members.)

Wrap-up

SAY: Throughout history, those who have known God well have come to sense the sanctity surrounding His name. Likewise, all of us who stay in contact with our creator will develop a richer and deeper understanding of His character. We will come to see, and perhaps even sing, as did King David, "O Lord our Lord, how excellent is thy name" (Psalm 8:l, KJV).

Discussion Questions

1. Why does God ask us to treat His name with respect?
2. What might be some reasons people feel compelled to misuse God's name?
3. The Christian is encouraged to pray "in God's name." What does this mean?
4. Reflect on what God has meant personally to you. What is a meaningful name/description of Him? (Example: One who comforts, etc.)
5. You have a coworker who considers himself a Christian. Nevertheless, he uses God's name on occasion to emphasize certain points during conversation. What would be an effective way to suggest that this is inappropriate?

Suggested Scriptures

Exodus 20:7; Psalm 8:1; Matthew 6:9.

Notes

____

____

____

____

____

____

____

____

____

[1] William Dyrness, Themes *in Old Testament Theology* (Downers Grove, Ill.: Inter-Varsity, 1979), p. 45.
[2] *Ibid.*, pp. 45-47.
[3] R. C. Sproul, *The Holiness of God* (Wheaton, Ill.: Tyndale, 1985), p. 148.

CHARITY

10
Trouble in Giver City

A Two-segment Simulation Experience on Assisting the Needy

PURPOSE

To develop a policy in harmony with Christian principles for responding to individuals requesting assistance (i.e., food, money, clothing). This program is designed to be presented at two consecutive meetings.

MATERIALS NEEDED

paper, pencils
laptop computer; printer is desirable
whiteboard or newsprint, marker

PREPARATION

Photocopy all of the cards found in the Board Meeting Materials section along with the instructions for the skit *Pastor Wellsford Meets the McNeedys.* Distribute these copies to selected individuals prior to the meeting. Give the participants a general idea of what the simulation experience will entail and their specific role in it.

Have the computer set up and ready for operation.

Trouble in Giver City Simulation: Part 1

Introduction

SAY (in the carefully modulated voice of a radio announcer): Polished glass and colorful neon suggest that all is well in the marketplace. But back alleys and nearby park benches tell another story—a tale of homelessness and hopelessness.

The Bible clearly calls us to provide for those in need. Accordingly, many Christian organizations devote themselves to assisting not only street people but also many other less-fortunate ones. These ministries demonstrate their Christian commitment by supplying food, clothing, shelter, and other necessities. If you ask those involved in this ministry, they'll tell you that they're simply following Christ's command to care for "the least of these" (Matthew 25:40).

Typically, the local church also attempts to reach out to those in need. Unfortunately, however, sometimes this caring body of believers is the target of tricksters and is taken advantage of because of their Christian generosity. The resulting tragedy of such dishonesty is that those who are truly in need may be denied assistance.

The simulation experience, Trouble in Giver City, is designed to help you through the process of formulating a Christian working policy that can guide your response to requests for assistance. Everyone has opinions about this, and, while a solution may not easily surface, we'll gain a greater appreciation for the complexity often involved in giving help to the needy.

Does a time ever come when a line must be drawn on Christian charity? Answering that question and furnishing guidelines for avoiding abuse in the realm of Christian generosity are what this program is all about.

Procedure

A. Skit: Pastor Wellsford Meets the McNeedys

Characters: *Pastor Wellsford*
Mr. McNeedy
Mrs. McNeedy
Parishioner

The actors, chosen from your group members, should have been informed previously of the basic plot and given at least a short time to discuss any details. A copy of the following may be furnished to the participants.

A destitute couple approaches the pastor of the Giver City Church in search of monetary assistance. The story line is flexible with the only requirement being that Pastor Wellsford makes the painful decision not to assist the couple because of insufficient proof of their need. This may be the result of a lack of credible references or some other reason.

A parishioner who has been waiting to speak with the pastor overhears the conversation and, after the McNeedys exit, proceeds to inform the pastor that he has not fulfilled his obligation as a Christian.

Unconvinced, Pastor Wellsford nevertheless agrees to bring up the matter of assisting the needy at the next church board meeting.

B. Board Meeting Simulation

The leader indicates that the church board meeting is about to convene. The audience is informed that *they* are church members in attendance at the board meeting. Also the group should be told that (if Position cards were distributed beforehand) there may be some audience opinions shared that are merely being role-played.

At this point the previously selected board members and other participants assume their various roles. The pastor, board members, and invited presenters take their places (preferably around a table). The pastor, also serving as board chair, informs the attendees of the problem. He then introduces each invited presenter and the board members. Each presenter is then allowed to briefly share their position/perspective of the problem, along with a suggested solution. The board members are then asked to do the same.

C. Discussion

The board chair opens the floor for discussion of the problem of assisting the needy, soliciting comments and potential solutions from the audience.

Note: from this point on, it is critical that the laptop computer operator specifically record relevant comments and suggestions.

During this discussion those holding Position cards will share their card's perspective of the situation. After ample discussion, indicate that the simulation portion of the program is over and move into the next segment. (Those holding Position cards may now be identified and can make clear their true positions, if different from their prescribed role.)

D. Debriefing Segment

Prior to exploring the scriptural record on the topic of assisting those in need, it is important to briefly evaluate the previous experience. This may be done by asking the following questions:

1. What were some of the strengths and weaknesses of the various perspectives or positions?
2. Was enough input supplied via the simulation to clearly portray the problem? If not, what additional information would have helped?
3. Did the simulation generally reflect realistic concerns? In what areas might it have been more authentic?

(For further discussion, see Discussion Questions section.)

Explain that the main objective of the experience was to show the three-way tension that often exists between charity, responsibility, and vulnerability, along with the difficulty involved in arriving at a viable solution.

Wrap-up (for Part 1)

SAY: We've seen the problem and many perspectives. Now the challenge is to refine our ideals into a viable, Bible-based philosophy for meeting needs. We'll work on that very thing next time we're together.

Trouble in Giver City Simulation: Part 2

E. Biblical Perspective

After briefly reviewing Part 1, begin with the following:

SAY: The importance of giving assistance to those in need is a major theme of Scripture. Perhaps the classic passage relating to Christian caring is found in Matthew 25:31-40. It's the first section of Jesus' parable of the sheep and goats and we're reading from the NIV.

"When the Son of Man comes in his glory, and all the angels with him, he will sit on his throne in heavenly glory. All the nations will be gathered before him, and he will separate the people one from another as a shepherd separates the sheep from the goats. He will put the sheep on his right and the goats on his left.

"Then the King will say to those on his right, 'Come, you who are blessed by my Father; take your inheritance, the kingdom prepared for you since the creation of the world.

For I was hungry and you gave me something to eat, I was thirsty and you gave me something to drink, I was a stranger and you invited me in, I needed clothes and you clothed me, I was sick and you looked after me, I was in prison and you came to visit me.'

"Then the righteous will answer him, 'Lord, when did we see you hungry and feed you, or thirsty and give you something to drink? When did we see you a stranger and invite you in, or needing clothes and clothe you? When did we see you sick or in prison and go to visit you?'

"The King will reply, 'I tell you the truth, whatever you did for one of the least of these brothers of mine, you did for me.' "

Caring for others has become a natural response to God's indwelling. But another side must be considered—the intriguing admonition recorded in Matthew 10:16. Here Jesus is preparing His disciples to take their message of redemption on the road. In so doing, He says, "I am sending you out like sheep among wolves. Therefore be as shrewd as snakes and as innocent as doves."

Such counsel may be appropriate for not only dealing with local councils and those in the "synagogue," but perhaps also when responding to potential recipients of Christian charity.

F. Needs Evaluation Document

This section of the program is designed to result in a simple set of guidelines to help concerned Christians be both selfless yet savvy in their giving to others.

The laptop operator should now read aloud the basic concerns, along with comments and suggestions that surfaced during the discussion segment of the program. (It is helpful if this data was organized and printed out—including photocopies, if necessary—for the group members.)

Using this information, along with the biblical insight just given and audience interaction, write on the whiteboard a sequential method for responding to requests for assistance by individuals apparently in need.

While a general statement of philosophy may be formed, the policy should also include (1) a sensitive method of evaluating needs, and (2) appropriate responses to specific concerns, such as where the most effective form of ministry lies (church, social service agency, etc.). Other concerns may also be addressed.

The laptop operator should enter the data and save the information for the final document. This may be printed out, photocopied, and distributed the following week. It may also be appropriate to supply a copy to the pastor for consideration.

Wrap-up (for Part 2)

SAY: Scripture is clear. As Christians, we must provide for those in need. But the Bible also leaves no doubt as to the value of exercising good judgment in all matters.

Because every situation is unique, a blanket policy on caring for the needy is insufficient. Accordingly, it seems appropriate that any request for assistance must be considered on an individual basis. The purpose of a bona fide set of guidelines to assist in that task is not merely to sift out the unscrupulous. More important, it helps assure that a legitimate need will not go unmet.

Today's disciples of Christ face a significant challenge in the realm of charity—the crossing of *compassion* for those whose earthly inventory is low with *wisdom from on high*. Such a hybrid can be grown in only one place: the greenhouse of God's grace. And the prayer of each "gardener" must be that the fruit produced might reflect His ultimate will.

Board Meeting Materials

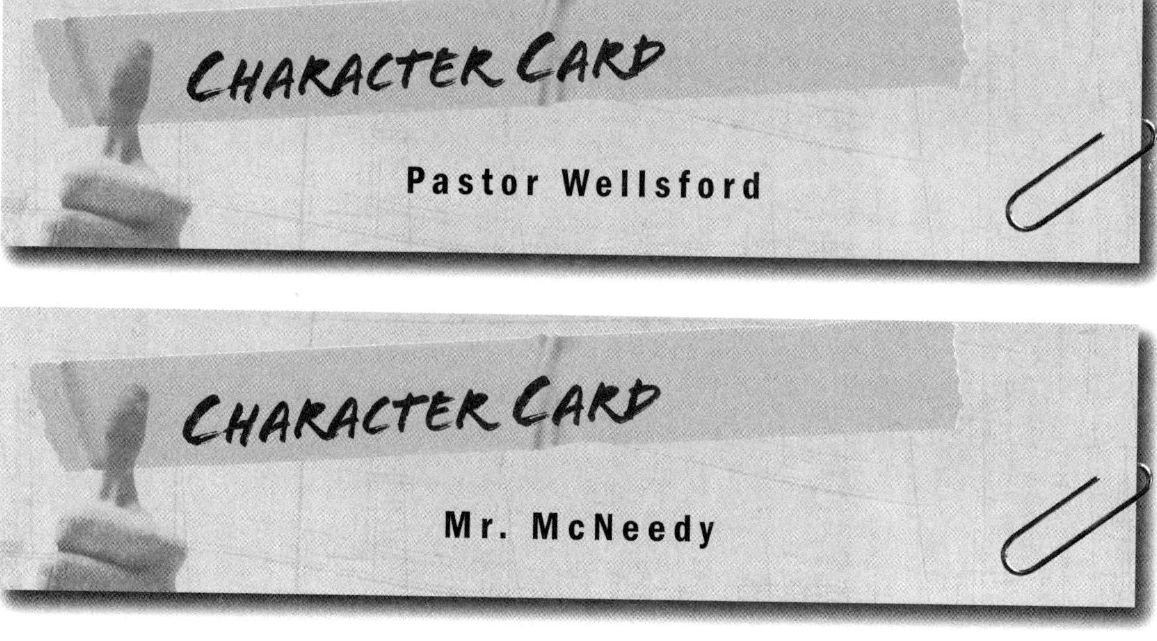

CHARACTER CARD

Mrs. McNeedy

CHARACTER CARD

Parishioner

INVITED PRESENTER CARD 1

__________________, director of Caring Heart Center for the Needy. Your concern for the less fortunate comes primarily from a position of moral, not religious, obligation. You subscribe to a philosophy of helping those who attempt to help themselves. Accordingly, your organization assists in the process of job placement.

A significant factor in Caring Heart's limited ability to assist the needy is the lack of both physical space and funds. You see increased governmental responsibility for caring for the needy as the most viable solution to easing the burden of private organizations.

Invited Presenter Card 2

_________________, assistant director of the city's social services agency. Your position on assisting the needy reflects the reality that inadequate government funding for those in need severely limits your agency's ability to meet the demand for assistance. While genuinely concerned for the less fortunate, you believe the ultimate solution is for churches and parachurch organizations to increasingly assume more of the responsibility for caring for the needy.

Invited Presenter Card 3

_________________, local citizen. You represent a strong faction of upper-income community members who believe that local taxation unjustly favors the poor. The corporate position of this group is a survival-of-the-fittest concept, with sociological natural selection an effective control to assure just distribution of wealth and material goods.

Board Member Card

Pastor Wellsford

As the senior pastor (and board chair) of the Giver City Community Church, you are besieged with requests for assistance. Your Christian belief in helping the poor is currently in tension with the fact that many of the church's welfare funds have been unwittingly distributed to professional panhandlers. Nevertheless, you remain committed to the idea of reaching out to those in need.

BOARD MEMBER CARD 1

You are vehemently opposed to any form of unreciprocated assistance. Your attitude is that anyone who is willing to work hard can find gainful employment and should thankfully do so.

BOARD MEMBER CARD 2

Concerning requests from the needy for financial help, you believe that it is not for another human being to judge the validity of that person's claims. You feel that Scripture prescribes an attitude of unconditional caring, thereby disallowing any form of discrimination such as a screening process to evaluate one's needs.

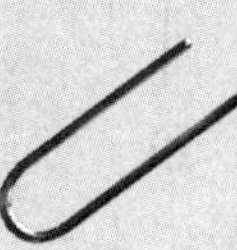

BOARD MEMBER CARD 3

Your opinion is that in today's uncertain world, financial contributions to organizations equipped to handle the needs of the less fortunate is the wisest choice for the Christian. This assures that funds will be used in the most efficient manner possible and avoids the many difficulties surrounding on-site requests for assistance.

Position Card 1

You believe that what life has robbed the unfortunate of should be supplied by those who are most able to furnish it. In other words, the wealthy.

Position Card 2

You believe only those who are willing to work should be rewarded with help. However, your position also holds that reimbursement should be in the form of necessities rather than cash. In your opinion, this helps avoid the possibility that the work arrangement is simply helping to support a vice or inappropriate lifestyle.

Position Card 3

You believe that government, local and federal, is primarily responsible for providing for the needy. The church's responsibility begins only when various social service agencies have been depleted of their resources.

Position Card 4

You believe that the church is most responsible for caring for those in need. Only when funds or other barriers prevent proper ministry to the unfortunate from taking place should government be called on for assistance.

Discussion Questions

1. Are the wealthy more obligated to provide for the needy than are those of lesser income? Why or why not?
2. What should be the "tangible" response of the person receiving charity?
3. Does the overall ministry of Jesus reflect any degree of selectivity in providing for the needs of others? If so, in what way(s) If not, how does His example work in today's world?
4. Agree or disagree: the capitalist philosophy is intrinsically wrong because it fosters inequality between the rich and poor. (Opinions should be supported.)
5. It has been shown that some street people are content with their lifestyle. What should be the attitude of the Christian toward such individuals?

Suggested Scriptures

Exodus 22:25-27; Deuteronomy 15:l-11; Proverbs 19:17; Matthew 7:1; 10:16; 25:31-46; James 2:15-17.

Notes

11
To Tell the Truth

PURPOSE

To learn how to effectively apply eternal principles of love and honesty to truthtelling (and other) situations requiring ethical choice. Norman Geisler's theory of graded absolutism is explored.

MATERIALS NEEDED

pencils, 3" x 5"cards

PREPARATION

none

Introduction

SAY: The truth and nothing but the truth. Living by that ethical creed should be second nature to every Christian. But because modern science and technology—and sin—have touched human existence, we face decisions that we wish we could avoid. The once cut-and-dried has become hazy, and some complex questions have no simple answers.

One area that has caused distress throughout the ages is truthtelling. While the situations change, a basic question remains: Are there rare times that honesty may not be the best policy? That's something we're going to soon consider. But first, a little fun!

Activity: *To Tell the Truth*

This exercise is based on the 1960s television program of the same name. Distribute an index card and pencil to members as they enter. Ask each to write down his or her name and a personal characteristic or event that no one else in the group is likely to be aware of. This might be an embarrassing moment, personal triumph, or any other singular experience.

Collect the cards and select one experience to be used during the first round of play. Ask the person whose experience is being used and two other individuals to step out of the room. The three are then informed of the experience selected and agree upon the introductory phrase they will use at the beginning of play. For example, if the true fact is that one of the three was once expelled from school, the common introduction spoken by each contestant in turn could be "I was once expelled from school."

On returning to the room, each person introduces himself or herself using the identical phrase, then sits down facing the audience. The audience then uses probing questions to determine which of the three actually belongs to the situation. (Asking directly if it is a certain contestant is not allowed.) The actual person answers truthfully, while the impostors respond as if they were the real person, making up details as necessary. After a given time or number of questions, the audience is asked to vote according to whom they believe is telling the truth.

Finally the moderator asks of the three, "Will the real person who was expelled from school [or other situation] please stand up?" After all feign standing, the actual person finally rises.

As used here, *To Tell the Truth* serves two purposes. First, it allows participants to learn more about each other. It also sets the tone for the ensuing look into the subject of truthtelling.

Bridge

SAY: *To Tell the Truth* contestants have been issued a temporary license to lie. But real life is hardly a game show. Because of its complexity, life holds ethical dilemmas. Whether or not to conceal the truth can be one of those.

Christians must base moral decisions—that includes truthtelling—on something deeper than today's horoscope. Certainly sound principles are necessary, and theories can prove helpful. But history has shown that morality in decision-making cannot ultimately be legislated for or dictated to another.

As creatures of free will we must make choices. To what extent this freedom can be exercised in good conscience has often been a matter of debate in Christian circles. Those who subscribe to the philosophy of situation ethics believe that love is the ultimate principle on which ethical decisions must be made. But who defines what love is in a specific situation?

Others are certain that prayer can provide the right solution to an ethical question. But praying fervently while deciding whether or not to tell a mugger about the $100 bill in your right sock would be quite a spiritual feat!

Still another group believes that ethical conflicts simply do not exist within the framework of God's sovereign will. Rather, the sinful human condition merely causes us to perceive a given situation as a moral dilemma.

Fortunately Scripture provides some significant insight concerning tough, ethically hazy situations that demand an immediate decision. But before considering the Bible's viewpoint, let's set the stage with a practical example of ethical tension.

Discussion: *Between a Rock and a Hard Drive*

Present the following situation to the audience: For the past two years you have been employed by IBX Business Systems in data entry. During this time a close friendship has developed between you and a coworker who is a single parent. You have learned that your friend's child has been diagnosed as having a rare disease that, if left untreated, will prove fatal.

Although there is a strict policy regarding the use of company equipment for personal gain, you have become aware that your friend has been doing this very thing to help pay off the mounting expenses related to her child's situation.

One day your supervisor discovers onscreen the remnants of one of your friend's freelance word processing jobs. She turns to you and asks, "Do you know who is responsible for this?" A yes will likely result in your friend losing her job, but replying no would be concealing the truth.

Look directly at your group and ask, "How would you respond, and why?" Allow for a brief discussion.

Biblical Perspective

SAY: The Bible doesn't have any word for us on freelance word processing. But it does contain several intriguing examples of individuals who faced an ethical dilemma that involved telling the truth. The first chapter of Exodus is a good example. Here we read that the Hebrew midwives had to choose between telling the truth and allowing the death of innocent children, or lying and saving their lives.

"The king of Egypt said to the Hebrew midwives, whose names were Shiphrah and Puah, 'When you help the Hebrew women in childbirth and observe them on the delivery stool, if it is a boy, kill him; but if it is a girl, let her live.' The midwives, however, feared God and did not do what the king of Egypt had told them to do; they let the boys live. Then the king of Egypt summoned the midwives and asked them, 'Why have you done this? Why have you let the boys live?' The midwives answered Pharoah, 'Hebrew women are not like Egyptian women; they are vigorous and give birth before the midwives arrive' " (Exodus 1:15-19).

They covered their actions with a lie, and babies lived. What is Scripture's response to this decision that seems so discordant with other biblical commands? (See Exodus 20:16; Proverbs 12:22; Ephesians 4:25; and others.) Again, the record is clear: "So God was kind to the midwives and the people increased and became even more numerous. And because the midwives feared God, he gave them families of their own" (Exodus 1:20, 21).

Thought Talk

SAY: It is perplexing to discover that God apparently affirmed an action that seems directly opposed to His moral will. But in his book *Options in Contemporary Christian Ethics,** Norman Geisler suggests why it may sometimes be so.

Geisler calls it graded absolutism. That's a mouthful. But graded absolutism is a name given to a system of ethics based on three main premises:

1. There are higher and lower moral laws.
2. Unavoidable moral conflicts do exist.
3. We are not guilty for what we can't avoid.

Several scriptures support the idea that not all moral laws are of equal weight. In Matthew 23:23 Jesus refers to "the more important matters of the law." In Matthew 5:19 and 22:36-39 Jesus speaks of the least and the greatest commandments.

Geisler maintains that because of the sinful reality of moral conflicts, in certain situations we must choose the higher moral law. In the case of the Hebrew midwives, the moral law of *mercy* took precedence over the moral law of *truthtelling*. Geisler believes that, having made their decision on such a basis, the midwives were not guilty. Likewise, we are not guilty in circumstances we cannot avoid.

Situation ethics is different from graded absolutism. Situation ethics downplays moral absolutes. Graded absolutism puts morality front and center. In situation ethics, the circumstances determine what is right and what is wrong. In graded absolutism the situation does not determine what is right. It simply helps us discover which moral principle applies.

So is there a place for a sanctified "white lie"? Graded absolutism would make it seem so. But can Christians accept this theory?

Ask participants to respond to the question of why or why not the theory of graded absolutism is viable. (See discussion questions.) Discussion of alternative theories may be appropriate. Also, application of theories to various hypothetical ethical dilemmas, including the situation previously described in *Between a Rock and a Hard Drive,* could prove enlightening.

Wrap-up

SAY: It might take divine intervention for us to agree regarding ethics in some situations, including truthtelling. Fortunately most of us don't usually find ourselves in situations like this. But even amid the haze of human dilemmas such as we've discussed, one thing remains clear: whatever ethical choices we make must be based on the eternal principles found in God's Word. Heaven will honor the fact that our decisions were made with more than mere human ideas in mind.

Discussion Questions

1. Can you think of a recent news story that involves ethical conflict? How did you react to that situation?
2. Some people would suggest that good intentions automatically absolve any moral guilt that may be associated with ethical conflict and decision-making. Is this correct? Why or why not?

3. Are there degrees of truth? If so, how would these categories be defined? (Some possible headings: fact, enhancement, deterrent, embellishment, deception.)
4. What is the difference between Christianity and morality? In ethical decision-making are the results the same for both? Why or why not?
5. In one sentence, define the point at which truth becomes a lie.

Suggested Scriptures

Joshua 2:1-7; 6:17; Proverbs 19:5; Micah 6:8.

Notes

---

* Norman Geisler, *Options in Contemporary Christian Ethics* (Grand Rapids: Baker, 1981).

FAITH

12
Exercise Your Faith

PURPOSE

To show the centrality of the person of Jesus Christ in the experience of faith. James Fowler's study of faith development is presented.

MATERIALS NEEDED

none

Introduction

SAY: If only I had more faith.

How many of us have been led to believe that the amount of belief that we have is the key ingredient in reaping good spiritual results? Such a perspective reminds one of Lewis Carroll's White Queen, who speaks to Alice in *Through the Looking Glass*:

"I can't believe that!" said Alice.

"Can't you?" the queen said in a pitying tone. "Try again: draw a long breath, and shut your eyes."

Alice laughed. "There's no use trying," she said, "one can't believe impossible things."

"I daresay you haven't much practice," said the queen. "When I was your age, I always did it for half-an-hour a day. Why, sometimes I've believed as many as six impossible things before breakfast."[1]

Without question, the Bible indicates that faith is an important part of the Christian experience. Scripture also shows that there is a connection between faith and miracles. But it is a narrow view that sees faith primarily as a spiritual muscle to be flexed in quest of the sensational. Rather, a richer, more mature perspective of faith comes when the focus shifts from results to a relationship.

Story Parable: Faith-ercise

READ ALOUD: Willard Newson, a recent convert, cheerily entered the sporting goods store at the local mall. "How may I help you today?" an athletic-looking salesclerk inquired.

"I'm here to pick out a few items so I can begin exercising my faith," Willard explained. The salesperson lifted an eyebrow as Willard retrieved a list from his jacket pocket.

"The first thing I'll need," Willard said, perusing the list, "is a helmet. I want to protect my head from rocks rolling down the sides of the mountains I'll soon be moving."

The salesclerk stifled a snicker. "I believe you mean climbing," he said.

"Well, that's a possibility too," Willard replied. "But I can use the same helmet for both." He looked around the store. "So, where are they?" he asked.

The confused clerk hesitated, eyeing Willard suspiciously. Nevertheless, he led the way past the fishing rods and hunting jackets over to the mountain-climbing gear. After selecting an attractive earth tone helmet, Willard again spoke to the clerk. "Next I'd like to see the swimwear," he said.

Just how a bathing suit would afford much defense against a rockslide the clerk could not fathom. But he showed Willard the available styles.

"This looks like a modest choice," Willard commented, considering a blue knee-length suit. "Not that I'll need it for long. But I'm bound to go under at least a time or two before I get the hang of walking on water." At this the salesclerk considered dialing mall security. But Willard's next request cut short this idea.

"The last thing I'll need to have a look at is your camping gear," he said. "Once my faith is in shape, I'll likely be swamped with requests—financial security, health, and happiness, that sort of thing. The locals won't be a problem, but I thought I'd pitch a few pup tents on the front lawn for the overnighters."

Bewildered, the salesperson once again paraded through the store, halting amid cookstoves, backpacks, and other outdoor items. Without speaking, he pointed to the tents. A quick about-face, and the perplexed salesclerk headed off in the opposite direction, muttering something about applying for work at the nearby health food store, where at least the nuts didn't talk.

Shortly Willard had selected several complementary tent styles that he would tastefully arrange around the new highlight of his landscaped yard—a recently installed electric fountain that he called Old Faithful.

Willard paid for his purchases and arranged for delivery of the tents. He hurried out the door. His last stop before beginning to exercise his faith was to be the Happy Hoe Garden Center. He still lacked a supply of mustard seeds.

Just as he reached the mall exit, Willard caught sight of a sign he had not noticed before. It read: Son Power Spiritual Fitness Center. Could providence be at work? Until now, he had been planning to exercise his faith at home, following the routine of a well-known television faith-erciser. But think of the high-tech equipment a professional training center must have! There'd be water-walking practice Jacuzzis, electronic monitoring of faith-to-doubt ratio, and computerized speedbag simulators for fighting the good fight. This would be faith-ercising at its finest!

Excited over the possibility, Willard headed over to sign up. Swinging open the narrow door, he stepped inside.

But to his surprise, the long room was empty. There was no equipment in sight. The only sign of life was a stream of light pouring through the cracks of a door at the far end of the room.

Just then the distant door opened, and out stepped a gentleman dressed in white. He walked toward Willard. Sensing his confusion, the man spoke.

"You're undoubtedly here to exercise your faith," he said. He held out his hand. "Welcome. I'm Gabe de Angelo, the assistant trainer."

Willard hesitantly shook the man's hand. "Uh, nice to meet you," he said. Then hoping to satisfy his curiosity, he commented, "I guess your rates must be pretty low here, since you don't seem to have much of anything to offer your clients."

Gabe smiled. "Well, the truth is we don't charge anything. As for the lack of exercise equipment, experience has shown that it's more of a hindrance than a help when it comes to achieving strong faith."

"I don't know," Willard protested. "With no training equipment, how can a faith rookie like me ever hope to become a big-time believer?" He then added, "Frankly, I'm not sure your way of exercising faith would even be worth trying."

Gabe de Angelo placed a hand on Willard's shoulder. Looking him straight in the eyes, he said, "Willard, our way is the only way. Once you're into the program, you'll begin to see that strong faith is not the result of trying. Rather, it comes by trusting in our Instructor and becoming more like Him."

A strange sense of conviction began to grow within Willard. After a brief silence he cleared his throat and spoke.

"I'd like to meet your instructor," he said.

"Follow me" came the quick reply. Gabe led Willard to the little room behind the door of which the bright light still shone. "Go on in, Willard. There are some others who came today too. But the Instructor has been waiting for you. He said He didn't want to begin without you."

A quizzical look crossed Willard's face. "But how—" Gabe cut Willard's question short. "Once you get to know Him better," he said, a twinkle in his eye, "you'll understand."

For some reason Willard believed him. He went into the room and sat down. It was to be the first of many evenings spent working out under the guidance of the Instructor.

To date, Willard hasn't moved Mount Everest or walked across Lake Tahoe. He hasn't had any calls for cures or cash, either. But if you ask him how his exercise program is going, he'll tell you he's certain that his faith is getting stronger every day.

Bridge

SAY: Faith is a fascinating topic. Let's find out more about what we believe.

Activity: *Belief Ballots*

This activity is designed to creatively elicit reflection and response concerning concepts found in the story *Faith-ercise.* Also presented for participants' reaction are general thoughts on faith.

Before reading the following statements on faith, designate three separate areas of the room as follows: one for those who agree, a second for those who think the statement is possibly correct, and a third area for those who disagree.

As each statement is read, have individuals move to the area that most accurately reflects his or her opinion regarding it.

After each "vote," randomly ask participants to tell why they chose the area that they did. (Tip: Those who make up the smallest areas after each vote often have more definitive and colorful comments than the others.)

True or False Questions for Belief Ballots

1. The essence of faith is more process than product.
2. A growing faith is an inevitable result of communion with Christ.
3. Faith, trust, and belief are different words describing the same thing. (Encourage definitions for each word, assuming some persons have disagreed.)

4. Faith in Christ is a purely spiritual matter.
5. True Christian faith will always be manifested by tangible evidence (see James 2:17).
6. "Life asks no questions that faith cannot answer."
7. Prayer plus faith equals power

Biblical Perspective

SAY: The Bible clearly indicates that faith is the mainstay of the Christian experience. The believer is encouraged by the fact that "with God all things are possible" (Matthew 19;26). But faith must be based on more than the miraculous. Scripture makes it clear that a mature, growing faith is rooted in a relationship with the Redeemer.

The eleventh and twelfth chapters of Hebrews contain significant insight regarding the issue of faith. Verse 1 of chapter 11 sets forth this definition:

Now faith is being sure of what we hope for and certain of what we do not see.

At first glance one might be led to the conclusion that the believer is asked to place his or her confidence in something for which there is no tangible evidence. The passage, however, smacks of conviction, as the words "sure" and "certain" suggest.

C. S. Lewis is helpful in providing a definition of faith that shows clearly the blending of the real with the intangible. He writes, "Faith is the art of holding on to things your reason has accepted as true, in spite of your changing mood."[2]

In a thought that relates to the logic of a person's faith, someone has said: "One's faith is only as good as the object in which it is placed."

The author of Hebrews has synthesized all of the above (and more) definitions of faith. He would have us know that while there is an element of the unseen involved, the Christian's faith is based on a series of well-grounded facts: that God became man, lived among us, died, and rose from the grave. That's why, following a listing of some of history's great men and women of faith, Hebrews 12:2 turns to faith's focal point: "Let us fix our eyes on Jesus, the author and perfecter of our faith."

Personal Application

As you discuss Fowler's stages of faith, encourage group members to consider where they are—or should be—in their faith journey. Point out the obvious, that the age span for each stage is approximate since individuals mature at slightly different rates depending on their heredity and life circumstances.

SAY: The book *Faith Passages and Patterns* refers to a study by James Fowler that provides insight concerning the broader, ongoing journey of faith.[3]

Stage 1: "God's just like my mommy and daddy."

Children from the ages of 2 to 6 come to think of God in the same way they view their parents. Images of God do not fit into a cohesive pattern, but children shape the necessary pieces into a framework that fits their needs.

Stage 2: "What's fair is fair!"

Justice is a central issue for those between the ages of 7 to 12. Stories are important, with the good guy winning out in the end the only acceptable option. As a result, the concept of grace for the bad guy can be difficult to grasp.

Stage 3: "I believe what the church believes."

This faith stage usually involves ages 13 to 18. It is a period of extreme self-consciousness. Accordingly, kids this age are significantly influenced by others' expectations and judgments of them, whether perceived or actually true. Indoctrination is effective, but it's only with great difficulty that believers in stage 3 are able to communicate *why* they believe what they do.

The interesting thing is that according to Fowler, *many Christians remain in stage 3 throughout their entire lives.*

Stage 4: "As I see it, God is . . ."

This is a stage of critical thinking and new ideas about God. How you think about God becomes important, not merely the content of your faith. It's a time of intellectualizing that, according to Fowler, may carry with it as much loss as gain. Yet it's necessary to reach this stage for your faith to continue to grow toward its ultimate goal.

Stage 5: "Don't confuse the map with the territory."

While stage 4 thinkers are concerned with having matters of faith "mapped out," as it were, with boundaries in place for the predictable journey, those in stage 5 sense that there is much to faith that they'll never really know. And so they develop a growing appreciation for mystery. Sacraments and other symbols of faith take on new meaning for them.

Stage 5 believers are also very open to dialogue and are willing to view faith from new perspectives. They have a maturity that comes by knowing God deeply and resting securely in His love.

Stage 6: I have a dream.

According to Fowler, very few reach this ultimate, last stage of faith. Using the phrase from Martin Luther King, Jr.'s famous civil rights speech, these "dreamers" are those who live out their lives in a quest to see the dream of the kingdom of God fully realized. To live in peace and harmony with one another and to represent God on earth is the call that these have heeded.

In conclusion, author Droege asks, Is one stage better than another? He answers by pointing out that if what you are looking for is a greater sense of worthiness in God's eyes, then no! Advancing on this ladder of stages does not make you more worthy to God. But, he adds, if you are striving for a more mature, self-fulfilling faith, then yes, reaching a higher stage of faith is better than existing at a lower one.

Wrap-up

SAY: Regardless of where you or I may be in our spiritual journey, it's important to remember the true source of abiding faith. Faith spurts may occasionally come to the Christian, and miracles actually occur. But it is through our everyday contact with Jesus Christ that our faith matures.

Are you feeling weak in the realm of belief?

There is no better time than the present to fall to your knees and begin to exercise your faith!

Discussion Questions

1. Why does God sometimes seem to delay responding to requests made in faith?
2. Is it possible for you to "exercise" your faith on a regular basis? If so, how?
3. Define and discuss the differences between faith and presumption.
4. How does Christian faith differ from secular faith, that is, faith in oneself, another person, or institution?
5. Some people would attribute a mountain-moving experience to fortunate timing rather than divine intervention. If you've had an experience that convinced you of God's personal touch in your life, what might be the best way to communicate this to someone who doesn't believe in God?

Suggested Scriptures

Habakkuk 2:4; Matthew 17:14-21; Mark 9:38-40; 2 Corinthians 5:7; Hebrews 11:1-12:2.

You might copy this simplified list of the stages of faith for each member of your group.

SUMMARY OF FAITH STAGES

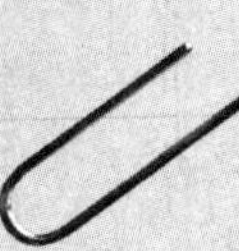

STAGE 1, AGE 2–6: "God's just like my mommy and daddy."
Children think of God in the same way they view their parents.

STAGE 2, AGE 7–12: "What's fair is fair!"
Justice is a central issue. They want the good guy to win, and have a problem grasping the concept of grace for the bad guy.

STAGE 3, AGE 13–18: "I believe what the church believes."
A period of extreme self-consciousness; influenced by others' expectations and judgments. Difficult to communicate *why* they believe what they do. Many Christians never go beyond stage 3.

STAGE 4: "As I see it, God is . . ."
Critical thinking and new ideas about God. *How* they think about God, not merely the content of their faith become imortant.

STAGE 5: "Don't confuse the map with the territory."
A realization that there's much to faith that they'll never really know. They appreciate the mystery of God and are willing to view faith from new perspectives.

STAGE 6: I have a dream.
They long to see the kingdom of God fully realized and seek to live in peace and harmony. They live to represent God on earth.

Notes

---

[1] W. Bingham Hunter, in *The God Who Hears*, quoting from Lewis Carroll's *Through the Looking Glass,* in *The Annotated Alice* (New York: Clarkson H. Potter, 1960), p. 251.

[2] C. S. Lewis, *Mere Christianity* (New York: Macmillan, 1943), p. 123.

[3] From Thomas A. Droege, *Faith Passages and Patterns* (Philadelphia: Fortress Press, 1983), chap. 3 ("Faith Seeking Understanding"), pp. 45-63. Fowler's study is patterned somewhat after Jean Piaget's stages of mental development and Lawrence Kohlberg's stages of moral development. As the result of his empirical studies, Fowler suggests that our faith develops in six basic stages through which we advance in a step-by-step process. However, as life continues we can revert to previous stages.

CREATIVITY

13
No More Closet Creativity

PURPOSE

To encourage development of God's gift of creativity.

MATERIALS NEEDED

pencils, paper for all

whiteboard or newsprint, marker

PREPARATION

Type or write on a piece of paper: Life is like . . .

Photocopy a page for each participant. These will be used in the activity *Life Is Like . . .*

Introduction

SAY: Murray Spangler was a department store janitor whose responsibilities included sweeping the long wooden aisles. Murray felt distressed at the inefficiency of the conventional broom and miserable because the dust he stirred up aggravated his asthma condition. There had to be a better way to clean the store's floors, he thought, and that's when the wheels of creativity began to spin.

Soon Spangler designed a crude contraption using a fan and his wife's pillowcase. It was faster and more effective than a broom, and actually sucked up dirt from the floor! Murray felt his newfangled grit-grabber might just prove to be the floor sweeper of the future.

But the inventive janitor knew that nobody would benefit from his product unless he found a way to put it into production.

Murray himself lacked enough money, but he knew of someone whose cash flow was considerably greater than his own. A meeting was arranged. The man recognized the massive potential of Murray's creation and agreed to sponsor its production.

You guessed it. Murray Spangler's brainchild, the vacuum cleaner, was destined for a glorious future. And Murray's investor, a man whose last name happened to be Hoover, would also clean up as the business grew and grew.

The Hoover logo on upright and canister models today is really a tribute to store janitor Murray Spangler. Our lives are made a little easier because he claimed the gift of creativity.

Bridge

Say: Who comes to mind when you think of creative people? Michelangelo? Picasso? Martha Stewart? Oprah Winfrey? Bono? Bill Gates? (Allow for audience response if desired.)

These people are certainly gifted with creativity. But every one of us on earth has been given the ability to create. Of course, we don't create *ex nihilo*, or "out of nothing," as God does, but we are still meant to experience the joy of self-expression through creative acts. Creativity is a gift of God.

Nevertheless, it's still hard for some of us to believe that we can be creative. So to demonstrate our creativity, let's try a little exercise. It's time to bring our gift of creativity out of the closet!

Activity: *Life Is Like . . .*

Distribute pencils and a prepared *Life Is Like . . .* slip (as noted in Preparation section) to each person. Have them complete the phrase Life is like a . . . They should then furnish another sentence of explanation. An example might be "Life is like a country road. The ride isn't always the smoothest, but if you stick with it, it'll take you where you need to go."

Encourage creativity! Instrumental background music is helpful. Work in pairs if desired.

After a few minutes, have group members read aloud their newly created metaphors.

Life Is Like . . . is a simple way to allow individuals to express themselves creatively. These phrases can also indicate the way various persons really do view life! (This background information can be helpful when ministering to specific group members.)

Bridge

SAY: Too often we view creativity as something reserved for those who are just a bit off-the-wall. Creativity, however, is not eccentricity. Rather, creativity is an expression of yourself that reflects God's personal, unique gifts to you.

To whose glory we use our creativity is another matter.

Typically, we may not think of Jesus as unusually creative. But in an article in *Discipleship Journal*, Sue Monk Kidd captures several colorful pictures of the creative Christ. Throughout His ministry Jesus often refused to conform to meaningless, ministry-restricting tradition. As Kidd points out, "Jesus related to people in a way that broke down tradition and opened doors to creative encounters."[1]

We're going to look at some ways that we might use our best creative efforts to God's glory. But first, let's quickly look at a few of the rewards of nurturing our God-given creativity.

Biblical Perspective

SAY: While the reasons for becoming a more creative person are many, some basic incentives include: (List these on a whiteboard or newsprint. If possible, have the list already written, ready to be referred to as you speak.)

Personal expression

There are times that a creative act can say something with much greater power than if the same thing could be expressed in words. That's why a forgiven woman once poured spikenard over the Savior's feet. What was the effect of this creative act? (Allow for your group to respond.) Jesus stated it clearly: "I tell you the truth, wherever the gospel is preached throughout the world, what she has done will also be told" (Mark 14:9).

Personal satisfaction and enrichment

The first chapter of the Bible portrays God as becoming increasingly satisfied with His creative efforts. Early acts of creation He called "good" (Genesis 1:10, 12, etc.), but by the sixth day we see that His joy is even greater. Now the splendor is called "very good" (Genesis. 1:31).

Just as God sighed with satisfaction at the end of Creation week, so you may enjoy the fruits and fulfillment of your creative labors.

Ministry value

No one was more creative in ministry than was Jesus. Just think of the numerous parables He told, each one so rich with meaning. And even more, think of His personal encounters and the way He often broke religious, traditional, and ethnic boundaries. Jesus made ministry happen—in places as colorful as near a small town well and in a fishing boat empty of fish. Creativity was one of the key ingredients to His effective ministry. It can be the same for you.

Spiritual growth

No one knew better the lasting effects of creative expression than King David. At different times of his life both music and poetry served as avenues of comfort and/or recommitment. David's creativity would last a lifetime, as Psalm 146:2 suggests: "I will praise the Lord all my life; I will sing praise to my God as long as I live."

Just as it did King David, creativity can help keep you and me in tune with our Creator.

Witness value

In today's fast-paced world, creative solutions to complex problems are in high demand. By providing creative, honest answers to this world's questions, the Christian glorifies God as the ultimate source of solutions. (See James 1:17.)

Bridge

SAY: As we look back through history we see many great creative acts. The pyramids of Egypt, the *Mona Lisa,* the airplane, the pacemaker, and the personal computer are just a few. But what about God's creativity? What are some of His most significant expressions of creativity past and present?

Invite participants to share ideas of what they believe are God's significant expressions of creativity.

Certainly creation reflects God's creative power. But Tim Stafford writes, "God's work is more than nature. He barely began there. People generally concede that you can know something about God through the universe He has made: 'The heavens are telling the glory of God.' But . . . God does not love stars as He loves me. The heavens, for all their splendor, will outlive their usefulness; they will be rolled up and taken away. So will the world we live in, for all its sensual glory and intricate ecology. They are like the scaffolding that Michaelangelo designed for painting the Sistine Chapel—marvelous in its own right, but dismantled at the proper time so that the great work could be clearly seen. When God had created everything else He went on to man and woman, creatures who sat up and talked to each other, who talked to Him. He has been working to complete these creatures ever since. He even became one. His people are God's great work, to be displayed in an entirely new setting—a new heaven and a new earth."[2]

Discuss and comment on the preceding. Is the author's basic premise correct?

Optional Activity: *Dreaming of Outreach*

Invite participants to share their responses as they complete this sentence: Something I would love to try as a new means of winning people to Jesus Christ is ____________________. Encourage everyone to be as *creative* and *specific* as possible.

Wrap-up

SAY: As we've seen, creativity is an avenue to personal fulfillment and a resource to help meet the everyday challenges of life. But it's also a vital tool of the heavenly "trade" of redemption. As Christians, we are called to be God's instruments in drawing the distracted to Jesus with our imagination and creative enterprise.

Why not begin stretching yourself for the sake of the gospel? Turn your creativity on for God. As Murray Spangler learned, your dream can make a difference.

Discussion Questions

1. In the arts the term *creative expression* is sometimes used in defense of overt sensuality and offensive display. For the Christian, what delineates true creative expression from artistic abuse?
2. What are some examples of creative expression found in Scripture?
3. You have just encountered a salty dockworker who ridicules your belief in God by saying, "It's foolish to talk to someone who never talks back, and to believe in someone you've never seen." What is the most creative response you can think of to these objections?
4. What are some specific ways a person might practice becoming more creative?

5. Creativity is an important ingredient in effective ministry. Give imaginative ideas for reaching out to others, and for the personal and corporate worship experience.

Suggested Scriptures

Genesis 1:1, 27; 2:19, 20; the parables of Jesus; 1 Corinthians 12:4-11.

Notes

___

___

___

___

___

___

___

___

___

[1] Sue Monk Kidd, "Living on the Creative Edge," *Discipleship Journal*, Issue 48.
[2] Tim Stafford, *Knowing the Face of God* (Grand Rapids: Zondervan, 1986), p. 177.

14
Vantage Points

PURPOSE

To show how viewing life from various perspectives fosters understanding of and empathy toward individuals' unique circumstances.

MATERIALS NEEDED

pencils, paper for all
whiteboard or newsprint, marker

PREPARATION

Draw an outline map of a "flattened" globe on the whiteboard or newsprint.

Prepare cards for the *Partial Pictures* activity.

Introduction

SAY: Some years ago William Least Heat Moon set out on an incredible cross-country journey. Despondent over a job loss and recent divorce, the Lakota and former college teacher decided that, in his words, "a man who couldn't make things go right could at least go."

So tucking his life savings of $428 under the dashboard of his van, Moon left Missouri and took to the road. He would cover more than 13,000 miles of United States highway before his return home. Moon didn't travel on the main thoroughfares and interstates. Instead, he chose the less-traveled highways, roads that at certain times of the day actually took on a mysterious cast of blue.

That singular feature would one day work to Moon's benefit. *Blue Highways* became the title of the best-selling book about his experiences on America's back roads. Along the way Moon discovered such diverse places as Remote, Oregon; Nameless, Tennessee; New Freedom, Pennsylvania; Why, Arizona; and Whynot, Mississippi.

The people he met were also colorful. There was Bill Hammond, a boat builder; Alice Middleton, a former school teacher and now octogenarian; and Brother Patrick, a Trappist monk who used to be a patrolman. Spending time with them, Moon came to know their stories.

Moon, on the final leg of his journey, stopped at a service station. He writes, "The pump attendant, looking at my [Missouri] license plate when he had filled the tank, asked, 'Where you coming from, Show Me?'

" 'Where I've been."

" 'Where else?' he said."*

The author's journey taught him a great deal about his native land. But more important, because of where he'd been he had shared in the essence of others' existence from their vantage point.

Bridge

SAY: Just as William Least Heat Moon experienced, where *we* have been can be a key to our being able to understand others. It's experiences—not geographical locations—that enable us to view life from another person's vantage point.

It can be frustrating, trying to understand people. But your own experiences provide you with a reference point. Whether it's joy, suffering, turmoil, or peace, these places of our hearts are keys that can unlock the doors of empathy and understanding.

When you have experienced anorexia nervosa, you do not so easily discount a friend's obsession with thinness.

When you have experienced abuse, another's bruises become a matter of deep concern.

When you have experienced the struggle of alcoholism, you are much more certain to affirm one fighting the same battle.

When you have experienced giving to those who have little, you resonate with those who live only to give.

And when you have experienced freedom in Christ, you celebrate more fully another's newfound commitment.

Where you've been and what you've experienced allows you to view life from another's perspective.

Biblical Perspective

SAY: There is no finer example of the life of experience than that of Jesus' life. Pick up any of the four Gospels and you'll see, woven throughout their pages, stories of His involvement in the lives of others.

Let's look at Luke 19. In very few words it captures Jesus taking advantage of an opportunity.

The Savior has spotted Zacchaeus perched up in a sycamore tree, looking down the street, waiting His approach. But Jesus was not content just to walk by and leave the tax man alone. Verse 5 begins, "When Jesus reached the spot, he looked up and said to him, 'Zacchaeus, come down immediately. I must stay at your house today.' " And so, Luke tells us, Zacchaeus "came down at once and welcomed him gladly."

But the Master's bed-and-breakfast choice rankled the self-righteous. "All the people saw this and began to mutter, 'He has gone to be the guest of a "sinner." ' "

Jesus, however, was not deterred. Reading on, we see that "Zacchaeus stood up and said to the Lord, 'Look, Lord! Here and now I give half of my possessions to the poor, and if I have cheated anybody out of anything, I will pay back four times the amount.' "

You can almost hear the cheers in that crowded house of old. And then Jesus, with love in His voice and a glint in His eyes, affirms the decision: "Today salvation has come to this house."

Zacchaeus had turned his heart toward heaven, and Jesus had been there to savor the experience.

Our Redeemer took many such highways and byways throughout His earthly existence. And He calls us to go where He has been.

Bridge

SAY: Limited experience in life makes it more difficult to view life from another's vantage point. It's as if you've moved to a foreign country without knowing the language. The end result is that we simply can't understand what's happening. But a broad base of life experience allows us to understand the most important vocabulary of all: the language of others' lives.

Of course, Jesus knew that sometimes it would be foolish for you to experience another's situation, even for the sake of ministry. We're not called to become drunkards so that we can minister to alcoholics. The Savior knew where to draw the line between associating with a friend and participating in the source of their struggle.

However, where experience falls short, information can fill in. Being informed on a variety of life issues is critical for the caring Christian. Ignorance helps no one, but learning what makes people tick can help us detect and meet needs in the tradition of Jesus Christ.

There are many different ways to get information; libraries, schools, seminars, and simply asking questions are just a few things that can help us learn to see from another's vantage point.

What kind of difference can being an informed Christian make in your life?

For one thing, it can help fill in the blanks of another's behavior or lifestyle. Here's how.

Activity: *Partial Pictures*

Write the following on the whiteboard or newsprint:

Arenas of Understanding

1. Dynamics of grief
2. Single parenthood
3. Cultural differences
4. Perfectionism
5. Religious convictions

Photocopy the following situations and distribute.

Perspective Card 1

Dynamics of grief

I just don't understand Celeste. Sure, losing a husband hurts. But she's so depressed all the time. If I were her, I'd buck up and get on with my life.

Perspective Card 2

Single parenthood

I've quit asking Roger to go anywhere with me. Ever since Laura left him and their son, for some reason all he can think about is work. I think he's trying to forget his pain by losing himself in his job.

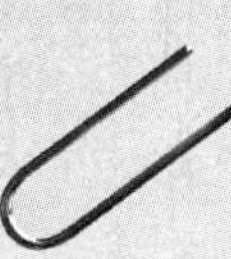

Perspective Card 3

Cultural differences

Could you believe it? I'll say this much—that's the last time we're going to invite a foreigner home from church for dinner. The outfit I could handle, but not his post-meal belching!

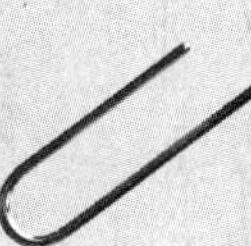

Perspective Card 4

Perfectionism

It's like the world has come to an end or something. Tracy gets a B in physics and she comes unglued. "It's the first time I've gotten a grade lower than an A," she wails. I say, "What's the big deal? Just forget it." Maybe it's time I found a new best friend. This one's driving me crazy!

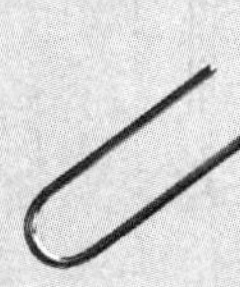

Perspective Card 5

Religious convictions

So there we are, out of gas on a Pennsylvania back road. Well, I walk up to this white farmhouse, knock on the door, and a bearded guy wearing suspenders opens it. I ask him if I can buy a little gas from him, just enough to get me to the nearest town. Get this! He tells me he doesn't have any! Can you believe it? A farmer without even a little can of gas? Well, right then I told him thanks for nothing and that I hoped everybody in Pennsylvania wasn't so unwilling to help out a stranger.

Narrator Bridges ***(for leader's use)***

1. Ignorance says that Celeste is a wimp. But informed on the dynamics of grief, you understand that . . .
2. Ignorance says that Roger is suppressing his emotions and withdrawing. But informed on single-parenting, you understand that . . .
3. Ignorance says that the belcher belongs in a barnyard. But informed on certain cultural characteristics, you understand that . . .
4. Ignorance says that a passing grade is enough. But informed on perfectionism, you understand that . . .
5. Ignorance says that the farmer is unfriendly. But informed on religious convictions, you understand that . . .

Photocopy the following clarification statements and distribute.

CLARIFICATION CARD 1

Dynamics of grief

Depression is an appropriate and expected dynamic in the experience of grief. Encouragement and support, not insensitivity are what Celéste needs.

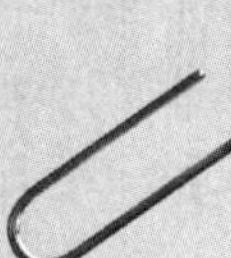

CLARIFICATION CARD 2

Single parenthood

Raising a child on a single income makes work a high priority in any single parent's life. And when Roger's not working, he knows that his son needs what time he has left.

Single parenting is tough, but Roger is making it. Affirmation should take the place of condemnation.

Clarification Card 3

Cultural differences

In the country where the visitor comes from, an after-dinner belch is considered a compliment to the host. No, it probably isn't something you want to make a future family tradition. Simply view it as a thank-you from the bottom of an appreciative belly.

Clarification Card 4

Perfectionism

For the perfectionist, anything less than the best is the worst. Perfectionism cannot simply be turned off when disaster strikes—it's an emotional disorder. Tracy needs to be shown—through unconditional love and acceptance, not rejection—that her personhood is not dependent on a perfect performance.

Clarification Card 5

Religious convictions

The Amish, many of whom live in Pennsylvania, choose a simple lifestyle. Their religious beliefs lead them to reject such modern conveniences as automobiles, power machinery, electricity, individual telephones, and other things that we take for granted. Obviously gasoline is missing on a farm that uses horses instead of tractors to plow the fields. Far from being unfriendly, the typical Amish person is, however, committed to their faith.

Here's how the activity works. Explain that a perspective growing from a position of ignorance will be read aloud. You will then bridge the perspective to a position of being informed, pointing to the Arena of Understanding, which can help clarify the true situation. Finally, the individual with the corresponding card will read their clarification statement aloud.

Example

1. First participant reads Perspective card 1 aloud.
2. Narrator refers to Arena of Understanding 1, Dynamics of Grief, then reads Narrator Bridge 1 aloud.
3. Second participant reads Clarification card 1 aloud.

Follow this succession for each of the remaining cards. *Partial Pictures* shows how being an informed Christian can give us the perspective we need to understand others more fully.

Wrap-up

SAY: In 1959 John Howard Griffin, a Caucasian, had his skin cosmetically changed to the dark hue of African-Americans. Griffin then went to live as a Black man in the southern United States. His book, *Black Like Me*, chronicles the prejudice he met and lived through as a result of his undercover work.

As Griffin learned, viewing life from another's perspective can produce pain. But sometimes an uncomfortable position is the most valuable vantage point. When we know how another is hurting, we are better prepared for the task of healing. Perhaps that is the most pointed advantage of learning to see from another's vantage point.

Discussion Questions

1. What is the ultimate purpose of learning to see from another's vantage point?
2. Besides the experience of Zacchaeus, what other biblical examples do we find of Jesus' experiencing the dynamics of different peoples' situations?
3. Does a time ever come when attempting to understand another's point of view becomes a worthless endeavor? If so, when?
4. Several arenas of understanding were mentioned in this program (cultural, religious).

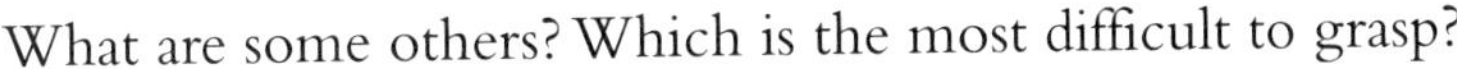

What are some others? Which is the most difficult to grasp?

5. Understanding another's point of view sometimes happens most effectively in a forum specifically designed to accomplish that purpose, such as contract negotiations. What basic principles from these kinds of corporate experiences can be applied to our personal quests for understanding?

Suggested Scripture

Psalm 8:1-5; John 11:32-35; Hebrews 4:15, 16.

Notes

* William Least Heat Moon, *Blue Highways* (New York: Fawcett Crest, 1982), p. 426.

work

15
Worship While You Work

PURPOSE

To consider work as a God-given arrangement, and thereby affirm its inherent dignity.

MATERIALS NEEDED

paper, pencils for all
hat or basket

Activity: *Jumbled Jobs*

As an icebreaker, have participants write their occupations in scrambled form on sheets of paper. For example, a secretary might write "ecrtysear." (Participants that are not currently working should answer with whatever occupies them throughout an average day. Also, students may wish to write the occupation they'd like to have when they finish school.)

Collect the slips in a hat or basket. Each member of the group draws one paper, attempts to unscramble it, and then gets out of their chair and locates the individual to whom it belongs. Instruct participants to ask that person to answer two questions: What do you like *most* about your job? and What do you like *least* about your job?

After a couple of minutes, regroup and solicit at random how various partners responded. *Jumbled Jobs* is designed to create a relaxed atmosphere and to direct attention to the topic of work.

Introduction

SAY: Work has many meanings. Some find deep joy and satisfaction in it. But others may consider work a necessary evil, something that can't be avoided because without it they can't pay for their existence. And then for some, work is merely an avenue to play. The paycheck will fill with thrills until Monday; then the cycle starts all over again. To still others, work becomes an escape from problems at home.

A lot of us find satisfaction in our workplace, but much of the world finds work less than fulfilling. Many share Mark Twain's view: "I do not like work even when someone else does it."

Of course, we live in a world that revolves around work. How does God want us to relate to it? A quiz may help answer that question.

Activity: *Work Wise*

Distribute pencils and paper to group members. Then ask the following questions aloud, allowing ample time for participants to write responses:

1. True or false: The primary objective of work is to make money.
2. Work is primarily a result of (a) the fall in Eden, (b) personal choices in the here and now, (c) societal expectations, (d) none of the above, (e) all of the above.
3. True or false: "Occupation" and "vocation" are two words that describe the same thing.
4. Fill in the blank: For the Christian, potential for ____________ in the workplace should be of primary concern.
5. The loss of their job is often most threatening to a person responding loss of (a) feelings of accomplishment, (b) community status, (c) self-identity, (d) self-worth.
6. True or false: Work is of more value than leisure.
7. Agree or disagree: "Those who work much do not work hard" (Henry David Thoreau).
8. Fill in the blank: ____________ is the key ingredient in job satisfaction.
9. Christian commitment demands that we pursue employment based primarily on (a) marketplace needs, (b) God-given abilities, (c) witnessing opportunities, (d) personal goals, (e) other.
10. True or false: Overall, the Protestant work ethic has been more of a help than a hindrance in fostering a balanced view of work.

Discussion

After the quiz, have group members "correct" their work. Ask respondents to raise their hands according to their answers. While most of the questions will have been answered somewhat subjectively, use the following to foster deeper discussion:

1. *The primary objective of work is to make money.* Questions: If this is true, why? If false, what should the primary objective be? Can the average worker's primary objective be anything other than monetary compensation? Would a worker in a developing country answer differently?

2. *Work is primarily a result of (a) the fall in Eden, (b) personal choices in the here and now, (c) societal expectations, (d) all of the above, (e) none of the above.* The biblical record suggests that "none of the above" would be the appropriate response. The curse that followed the entrance of sin into the world merely introduced the elements of difficulty and struggle into human labor (see Genesis 3:17). According to Genesis 1:28, Adam and Eve were assigned the task of managing God's creation from the beginning. Question: What might have been the purpose of work prior to the Fall?

3. *"Occupation" and "vocation" are two words which describe the same thing.* While both words can relate to work, the word "vocation" comes from a word meaning "a calling." Could your occupation be different than your vocation? Why or why not?

4. *For the Christian, potential for ______________ in the workplace should be of primary concern.* Discuss options, which might include: advancement, ministry/witnessing, personal growth, professional growth, increased income. Question: Is the pursuit of any of these wrong?

5. *A job loss may threaten an individual most because of the corresponding loss of (a) feelings of accomplishment, (b) community status, (c) self-identity, (d) self-worth.* Both (c) and (d) would probably be root issues for someone experiencing a job loss. Self-identity in particular can be shaken, as one's entire existence often revolves around his or her work. Questions: Is having your self-identity so closely tied to work a healthy thing? How can you appropriately disassociate yourself from work?

6. *Work is of more value than leisure.* Tim Hansel points out that the Latin word for "leisure" was *licere*, which means "to be permitted." The Latin word for "work" on the other hand, was *negotium*, which is translated "nonleisure." In other words, as they are related to each other work, was actually secondary to leisure. Hansel also points out that the Greek word for "leisure" was *ascholia*, which leads to the English word for "school." In the Greek world, leisure was a time for learning.[1] Question: Given the aforementioned definition of "leisure," what are some ways that a Christian might spend genuine leisure time?

7. *Agree or disagree: "Those who work much do not work hard"* (Henry David Thoreau). Question: What do you think Thoreau was suggesting by this statement? If you agreed, why? If not, why not?

8. *Fill in the blank:* ____________ *is the key ingredient in job satisfaction.* Question: Would this key likely be different for the Christian and non-Christian? If so, in what way(s)?

9. *Christian commitment demands pursuing employment based primarily on (a) marketplace needs, (b) God-given abilities, (c) witnessing opportunities, (d) personal goals, (e) other.* The criteria for landing a job may be more complex than one primary consideration. Ask for respondents to tell why they answered as they did, particularly those who selected "other." Question: Should job-hunting be geared around our own or others' needs? In what way(s)?

10. *True or false: Overall, the Protestant work ethic has been more of a help than a hindrance in fostering a balanced view of work.* The Protestant work ethic basically suggests that work is of God, and as such should be embraced with zeal and diligence. Question: If true, in what ways has this perspective been helpful? If false, how has it been harmful?

Bridge

SAY: No amount of discussion can change one fact—our work is still with us. To discover how our work can work *for* us, let's look at the Good Book.

Biblical Perspective

SAY: There's no question that we're called to live responsibly. This involves work, as the apostle Paul states in 1 Thessalonians 4:11, 12: "Make it your ambition to lead a quiet life, to mind your own business and to work with your hands, just as we told you, so that your daily life may win the respect of outsiders and so that you will not be dependent on anybody."

Paul is even more direct in 2 Thessalonians 3:10, where he quotes a rule: "If a man will not work, he shall not eat."

But the biblical call to work is not a summons to misery. The book of Ecclesiastes sets forth a valuable perspective on work. In the third chapter, beginning with verse 12, the author writes, "I know that there is nothing better for men than to be happy and do good while they live. That every man may eat and drink, and find satisfaction in all his toil—this is the gift of God."

Here is the scriptural balance then: to work, but to whenever possible enjoy your work, knowing that it is a gift of God.

Because work is heaven-sent, it has an inherent dignity. From homework to housework to every legitimate work, no work is menial in the eyes of God. True, not all employment is fun. Of course, a fulfilling job is the ideal, and there are very good reasons to try to find work that you enjoy.

Nevertheless, the reality is that work can be less-than-heavenly. But as Christians, whatever our occupation, we are through our jobs doing the work of Christ on earth. Not merely as His witnesses, but as living tools used of Him to accomplish His sovereign will. How? Doug Sherman describes one way in his book *Your Work Matters to God*. He writes:

"A friend of mine operates a pallet company. Pallets are the platforms used extensively in the transportation industries, designed to make it easier for forklifts to load and unload stacks of goods. My friend's company manufactures these pallets.

"Now, how could my friend's pallets possibly fit into the work of God in the world? Actually, they are an important, albeit humble link in a complex chain that God uses to meet my needs and your needs. Those pallets are an indispensable part of the trucking industry—an industry that delivers ruby-red grapefruit from the Rio Grande, boxes of cereal from Battle Creek, Michigan, and milk from Coppell, Texas, to a supermarket near my home.

"All of these come together at my family's breakfast table. Before we eat, one of my children thanks God for the food. Why? Because He has brought to our table something we need. . .

"Did you notice my friend's pallets? They were tucked away under those crates of grapefruit, boxes of cereal, and gallons of milk. Though [they were] obscure, God used them to meet my family's needs."[2]

In large, small, and sometimes even unseen ways, each of God's children contributes to the uplifting of humanity through his or her job. Knowing that, we can tackle our tasks with joy, even amid the curse of toil. When we offer our best efforts back to God, our work stations become places of worship.

Wrap-up

SAY: It seems unlikely that work, a responsible return of our abilities to God, will ever be a thing of the past. Yes, the curse will be lifted in heaven. But knowing God more deeply will likely continue to happen in many ways, including through the fruits of our labors.

From plants grown under our care to the study of the universe, the pursuit of understanding God will go on. Happily, such "work" will be nothing short of sheer pleasure.

Discussion Questions: *See Activity: Work Wise*

Suggested Scriptures

Genesis 1:26, 28, 29; 2:15; Ecclesiastes 3:12; 5:18; 1 Thessalonians 4:11, 12.

Notes

[1] Tim Hansel, *When I Relax I Feel Guilty* (Elgin, Ill.: David C. Cook, 1979), p. 30.
[2] Doug Sherman and William Hendricks, *Your Work Matters to God* (Colorado Springs: NavPress, 1988), p. 89.

MIXERS

Group Mixers

MIXERS:

Short activities designed to foster an atmosphere of warmth, acceptance, and equality in your meeting.

BENEFIT:

Provide opportunities for group members to learn new things about each other.

Try one of these mixers at the beginning of your next gathering. Along with completing the specific task for each mixer, regular attendees should introduce themselves to newcomers and make them feel welcome.

Activity 1 Participants find and greet all other individuals whose birthday is during the same month as their own. If someone who does not share a birthday month with anyone there is present, all group members converge on that individual with words and gestures of welcome!

Activity 2 Count the group off by fours. Same numbers get into a huddle and tell each other an important "discovery" made during the past week.

Activity 3 Allow two minutes for each person to learn the favorite foods of others in their group. The person able to recall the most receives a food prize, such as a cookie, cupcake, or brownie.

Activity 4 During a specified time period participants find people they haven't seen since the last meeting, and shake hands with them.

Activity 5 Count off the group using the following designations: (1) boat, (2) plane, (3) car, and (4) train. Same-designation persons greet each other, then describe their favorite place to visit.

Activity 6 Participants greet five others in the room using (in sequence) the following one-word greetings: (1) so (2) nice (3) to (4) see (5) you. Those who have been greeted by the word "you" must tell a highlight from their past week.

Activity 7 Count the group off using the following categories: (1) cover, (2) title, (3) page, and (4) index. Members of individual categories greet each other, then tell an insight or other highlight gleaned from a book or article they've recently read.

Activity 8 Each group member finds an initial partner with whom to share the information requested in the first round of this experience. When the words "Dooka, Dooka" are called out by the leader, partners share with each other the information requested by the leader. When the leader again calls out, "Dooka, Dooka," participants find a new partner, and they share with each other the new information requested by the leader. This pattern continues for as many questions as the leader asks. Following are some sample "Dooka, Dooka" questions. (Allow between 30 seconds and one minute for each question to be answered.)

If you could live anywhere in the world, where would it be, and why? Who is a particularly intriguing historical character to you, and why? What is your favorite Bible story or verse?